978-3667-1140·37

PORSCHE

INTRO

Neulich zwischen Bunyola und Sóller, im verbissenen Infight mit dem Serpentinen-Inferno des Coll de Sóller, vollkommen aufgelöst im glückseligen Stakkato von Anbremsen, Luftholen, Einlenken, Verharren im Scheitelpunkt-Schwebezustand, Luftanhalten, Auslenken, Ausatmen, Beschleunigen. Plötzlich zarter Haftungsabriss an der Hinterachse, minimales Gegenlenken und gleichzeitig ein herrliches Bergpanorama im Blick. In dieser köstlichen Millisekunde hatten wir eine Eingebung: Wir wollen jetzt nicht behaupten, dass die meisten Menschen Mallorca aus den falschen Gründen lieben, sind aber fest davon überzeugt, dass es auf diesen 3600 Quadratkilometern im westlichen Mittelmeer mehr zu entdecken gibt, als gemeinhin bekannt ist. Mallorca ist einsam und vielschichtig, erhaben und schroff, mächtig und voller Spannung. Die Straßen gehören zum Besten, was man mit Asphalt anstellen kann, sie sind ein Fest des *Soulful Driving*. Muss man für Mallorca eigentlich noch eine Lanze brechen? Muss man wirklich erzählen, wie großartig diese Insel ist? Einen Moment lang war uns klar: Ja! Denn wo sonst sollten wir Soulful Drivers sein wollen. In Momenten wie diesem. Wenn nicht hier.

—

Recently between Bunyola and Sóller, in a bitter infight with the serpentine inferno that is the Coll de Sóller, utterly immersed in the blissful staccato as I brake into the corner, breathe in, turn in, hang on to the apex for a moment as time stands still, hold my breath, release the steering, breathe out, accelerate. Suddenly, there's a slight loss of grip at the rear end – a tiny countersteer and, at the same time, a stunning mountain panorama reveals itself. It was in this delectable millisecond that we felt it. We're not trying to suggest that most people love Majorca for the wrong reasons, but we are absolutely convinced that there is far more to discover on these 3600 square kilometres in the western Mediterranean than is commonly known. Majorca is out-of-the-way and complex, sublime and rugged, abundant and full of energy. The roads are among the best that asphalt has to offer; they are a festival of *Soulful Driving*. Do we really need to argue the case for Majorca? Do we really need to explain how great this island is? For that brief moment, there was no doubt in our minds – yes! Where else should Soulful Drivers want to be in moments like this, if not here?

COLL SA CREU

**ETAPPE
STAGE**

**ETAPPE
STAGE**

Die erste Etappe auf unserer Mallorca-Runde widmet sich dem sonnigen Südwesten der Insel und der Serra de Tramuntana. Wir starten in der ebenso turbulenten wie geschichtsträchtigen Hauptstadt Palma de Mallorca, streifen dann die Küste entlang nach Südwesten und statten den bildschönen Fischerdörfern Sant Elm und Port d'Andratx einen Besuch ab. Von hier geht es zuerst ins Landesinnere, dann über die Berge der Tramuntana an die Westküste. Wir folgen der Küstenlinie bis Banyalbufar und erforschen nun den Gebirgszug auf einem Loop im Inneren zurück bis Andratx. Die Runde wird bei Banyalbufar wieder abgeschlossen, auf den nun folgenden Kilometern bis Valldemossa lassen wir die erste Tagesetappe ausklingen

The first stage of our journey around Majorca is dedicated to the sunny southwest of the island and the Serra de Tramuntana. We start in the capital, Palma de Mallorca – as turbulent as it is historic – head southwest along the coast and pay a visit to the picturesque fishing villages of Sant Elm and Port d'Andratx. From here, we turn inland then over the Tramuntana Mountains to the west coast. We follow the coastline to Banyalbufar and explore the mountain range on an inward loop that takes us back to Andratx and ends at Banyalbufar again. We then enjoy a relaxing end to day one on the remaining kilometres to Valldemossa.

Auf der zweiten Etappe beschäftigen wir uns hauptsächlich mit dem zentralen Teil des Gebirges der Serra de Tramuntana. Vom Start in Valldemossa bewegen wir uns zuerst noch einige Kilometer mit großartiger Aussicht auf das Mittelmeer in Richtung Sóller, ab hier verläuft die Route aber hinein in die Berge. Über das Gebirgsstädtchen Fornalutx und eine zweimalige Tunnel-Unterquerung des Puig Major-Massivs gelangen wir wieder zurück ans Meer. Vorher darf aber die schmale Serpentinen-Strecke nach Sa Calobra genossen werden, die besonders außerhalb der Touristen-Hochsaison oder am frühen Morgen und späten Abend puren Fahrspaß und Kurven satt bietet. Von hier aus überqueren wir das Gebirge erneut, halten uns dann in den Hügeln am Fuß der Tramuntana zurück nach Südwesten, um zusammen mit der alten Eisenbahn aus Palma de Mallorca die Runde nach Sóller abzuschließen. Ein abschließender Loop nach Nordosten schließt die Runde ab und bringt uns zum Ausgang der zweiten Etappe beim Kloster Lluc.

On the second section of our journey, we cover mainly the centre part of the Serra de Tramuntana mountain range. From our starting point in Valldemossa, we first spend a few kilometres heading for Sóller with an amazing view of the Mediterranean, after which the route leads into the mountains. We return to the sea via the mountain village of Fornalutx and two tunnels through the Puig Major mountain. But first, we were able to enjoy the delights of the narrow Sa Calobra serpentine, which offers sheer driving joy and curves galore, especially out of the main tourist season or in the early morning or late evening. From here, we cross back over the mountains then linger in the hills at the foot of the Tramuntana heading southwest again to complete the loop to Sóller, after crossing the Coll de Sóller, alongside the old railway line from Palma de Mallorca. We finish the tour by looping to the northeast and ending the second stage at the Lluc Monastery.

**ETAPPE
STAGE**

**ETAPPE
STAGE**

Nachdem uns die Serra de Tramuntana für die ersten beiden Tagesetappen intensiv begleitet hat, lassen wir das Gebirge im Westen Mallorcas auf der dritten Etappe endgültig hinter uns. Der Ausklang dieser großartigen Landschaft kann allerdings gebührend gefeiert werden: Mit den Kilometern zum Kap Formentor am nördlichsten Zipfel der Insel liegt noch einmal ein höchst intensiver und landschaftlich reizvoller Streckenabschnitt vor uns, der – hin und zurück – gleich zweimal absolviert werden muss. Von hier aus rollen wir in die nördlichen Ausläufer der großen, zentralen Ebene Mallorcas hinein, halten uns stets an der Küste und landen zum Ende der Etappe in den Bergen der Serres de Llevant. Die sind zwar nicht so hoch und rau wie das Tramuntana-Gegenstück, haben aber ihren ganz eigenen, milden Reiz. Schluss der Etappe ist nach einem Besuch der Tropfsteinhöhle von Artà beim Städtchen Porto Cristo, etwas nördlicher der hier gelegenen Drachen-Höhlen „Coves del Drac".

After the intense companionship of the Serra de Tramuntana on the first two days, we finally leave the mountain range on the west side of Majorca behind us on the third stage. The finale delivered by this fantastic landscape is nevertheless a fitting celebration. The kilometres to Cap de Formentor on the northernmost tip of the island offer yet another intense and scenically stunning piece of road, which – there and back – simply has to be covered twice. From here, we roll into the northern foothills of Majorca's great central plain, sticking resolutely to the coast and ultimately completing the stage in the mountains of the Serres de Llevant. They may not be quite as high and rugged as their Tramuntana counterparts, but nevertheless have their own, gentler appeal. Following a visit to the Caves of Artà, we reach the end of the stage at the small town of Porto Cristo, a little north of the "Coves del Drac" (Dragon Caves).

Die vierte und letzte Etappe einer Mallorca-Umrundung führt über die Hügel-Landschaft der Region Llevant im Nordosten, entlang des Meers im Osten mit seinen Tropfsteinhöhlen und der zerklüfteten Küste, danach bleibt der Rückweg zur Inselhauptstadt Palma durch die flachen Ausläufer der zentralen Ebene. Verglichen mit der spektakulären und rauen Gebirgslandschaft im Westen scheint diese Etappe deutlich abzufallen, kann aber trotzdem ihre Reize entfalten. Wer sich Zeit für die kleinen Fischerdörfer, Klöster und Eremitagen in den Hügeln nimmt, entdeckt ein Mallorca mit reduzierter Geschwindigkeit und sehenswerten Ecken. Die Fahrt ins Landesinnere ist nicht nur wegen eines Abstechers zum zentral gelegenen Puig de Randa lohnenswert, sondern auch, um einen Eindruck vom Charakter der Zentralebene zu erhalten: Ohne die einsilbige Atmosphäre dieser Landschaft ist das Bild von Mallorca unvollständig, sie nimmt einen großen Teil der Inselfläche ein. Mallorca ist mehr als Tourismus und Freizeit – das wird in dieser landwirtschaftlich stark genutzten Gegend zum Anfassen deutlich. Ein ehrliches Land.

The fourth and final stage of a tour around Majorca takes us over the hilly landscape of the Llevant region in the northeast, along the sea in the east, with its caves and rugged coastline. After that comes the road back to the island's capital, Palma, through the low foothills of the central plain. Compared with the spectacular and rugged mountain landscape in the west, this section seems like quite a come-down, but is nevertheless able to reveal its own appeal. If you take time to explore the little fishing villages, monasteries and hermitages in the hills, you discover a low-speed Majorca and plenty of corners worth seeing. The drive to the middle of the island is worthwhile not only for a detour to the central Puig de Randa but also to gain a feel for the character of the central plain. Without the monosyllabic atmosphere of this landscape, the image of Majorca is incomplete. It occupies a large proportion of the island's surface. Majorca is more than tourism and leisure – something that becomes patently obvious in this heavily agricultural region. A simple, honest land.

EDITORIAL

Mallorca? – Ja, tatsächlich, Mallorca. Keine Lust auf Erklärungsbedarf, aber vermutlich muss das sein. Denn: Diese Insel polarisiert. Sie ist zu einer Karikatur geworden – und das zu Unrecht. Perspektive eins zeichnet ein schockierendes Bild von der Hauptsache-billig-Sonne-All-Inclusive-Mentalität unglaublicher Touristenmassen, die jeden Sommer die Insel fluten wie eine biblische Heuschreckenplage, den alkoholbefeuerten Vergnügungs-Exzessen des Massentourismus, der Gentrifizierung ganzer Viertel und Gegenden oder dem AirBnB-Ausverkauf privaten Wohnraums. Perspektive zwei schottet sich in rührseliger Finca-Romantik ab, preist auf naivem Gefühls-Autopilot die unberührte Schönheit vieler Ecken Mallorcas und biedert sich mit betulichem Insider-Selbstverständnis als Insel-Versteher an. Frei nach dem Motto: So schlimm ist das doch alles nicht. Irgendwo dazwischen finden sich dann noch die Auswanderer, die vermutlich irgendwann beim Sangria das Gefühl bekommen haben, Mallorca könne eine prekäre Existenz in eine Erfolgsgeschichte verwandeln und ihr krachendes Scheitern in der Fehleinschätzung eigener Originalität auch noch fürs Reality-TV dokumentieren lassen.

Ist das Mallorca? – Ganz bestimmt nicht. Es darf aber festgehalten werden: Hier läuft etwas gewaltig schief, die Tourismus-Maschine überhitzt und die Mallorquiner tun ganz recht daran, sich immer mehr gegen den Ausverkauf ihrer Insel zu wehren. Das eigentliche Problem ist aber, dass Mallorca zwischen allen Stereotypen nur noch schwer zu erkennen ist und in der öffentlichen Wahrnehmung regelrecht schizophren präsentiert wird. Entweder wird nur über Probleme gesprochen oder man blendet sie gezielt aus. Vielleicht geht das auch gar nicht anders, wenn man als bestimmende Perspektive den analysierenden Blick von außen wählt. Es könnte deshalb ganz gut sein, und legitim obendrein, sich keinem dieser Blickwinkel anzuschließen. Einen Schritt zurück in respektvollen

Majorca? – yup, really, Majorca. I don't particularly want to explain it, but I suppose I'll have to. This island has a polarising effect. It has become a caricature of itself – unfairly so. Perspective one is a shocking image of the cheap-all-inclusive-sunshine mentality of the heaving throngs of tourists who flood the island every summer like a biblical plague of locusts, the alcohol-induced excesses of mass tourism, the gentrification of entire neighbourhoods and communities and the AirBnB sell-out of private property. Perspective two cloaks itself in sentimental finca-romanticism, applying a naïve emotional autopilot to extol the unsullied beauty of many parts of Majorca with the ingratiating pseudo-insider knowledge of a would-be local – very much with a sense of "it's not as bad as all that". Somewhere in between languish the expats who, presumably in a sangria-soaked haze, concluded that Mallorca could transform a precarious existence into a success story and, in a misjudgement of their own originality, go on to have their crushing failure documented for reality TV.

Is that Majorca? – definitely not. However, it's important to note that something is going seriously wrong here – the tourism machine is overheating and the Majorcans are, quite rightly, increasingly defending themselves against the complete sell-out of their island. But the problem is that the real Majorca is very difficult to spot among all the stereotypes and has the public persona of a true schizophrenic. The problems are either the only topic of discussion or they are carefully and diligently masked out. Maybe there's no other way when you choose external analysis as the defining perspective. It may therefore be no bad thing – legitimate, even – to adopt none of these points of view but instead to distance oneself with a respectful backward step. For non-Majorcans, there is one overriding truth – Majorca does not belong to us. Nothing can change that – regardless of those warm-and-fuzzy vacation feelings,

Abstand zu gehen. Für Nicht-Mallorquiner gilt nämlich vor allem eines: Mallorca gehört uns nicht. Daran ändern auch wohlige Urlaubsgefühle nichts, gefühlsüberfrachtete Erinnerungen oder der Eindruck nach soundso vielen Sommerferien auf der Insel irgendwie dazuzugehören. Mallorca ist eine fremde Gegend – wie übrigens so ziemlich jeder Ort auf der Welt –, die man am besten mit Respekt und Faszination entdeckt. Ohne den nötigen Abstand wird man kurzsichtig. Deshalb die Fakten aus dem CURVES-Cockpit: Mallorca ist die größte Insel der Balearen-Gruppe im westlichen Mittelmeer. In Ost-West-Richtung rund 100 Kilometer breit und von Norden nach Süden 80 Kilometer lang, mit einer Küstenlinie von etwas mehr als 550 Kilometern. Das Wetter ist im Sommer heiß und sonnig, im Winter mild und gelegentlich regnerisch. Geologisch liegt Mallorca zusammen mit den anderen Balearen-Inseln (Menorca, Ibiza, Formentera und über 140 weiteren, unbewohnten Inseln) auf der Iberischen Platte, politisch gehören die Balearen als eine autonome Gemeinschaft zum Königreich Spanien, der auf Mallorca gesprochene mallorquinische Dialekt ist eine Form des Katalanischen. Nach einer steinzeitlichen Besiedlung aus Iberien und der heutigen Provence konnte sich Mallorca lange Zeit unter dem Radar der großen europäischen Geschichte halten, eine Phase in Zugehörigkeit zum Reich Karthagos ist ebenso hervorzuheben wie der spätere Wechsel ins Römische Reich. Es folgen maurische und normannische Einflüsse ebenso wie die jüngere Zugehörigkeit zu Spanien – prägend bleibt aber die mallorquinische Kultur. Typisch für Inseln. Man lässt kommen und gehen, man bleibt.

Wer mit offenen Augen nach Mallorca kommt, wird diesen herben, selbstbewussten Charakter schnell erkennen und schätzen lernen. Er ist wie die Landschaft der Insel: Raue und ursprüngliche Gegenden machen sie im Wesentlichen aus. Gleich hinter Palma, S'Arenal und Magaluf breitet sich die Pla de Mallorca ins Landesinnere aus, eine im Sommer brütend heiße Ebene mit derbem landwirtschaftlichem Charakter, so ehrlich wie der schwielige Händedruck eines Mandelbaum-Bauern. Zum Nordwesten hin folgt die Region Es Raiguer, das Hügelland am Übergang in die Serra de Tramuntana mit ihren über 1000 Meter hohen Bergen. Wild und einsam schafft es der Westen Mallorcas achselzuckend und unberührt vom Entertainment-Tourismus selbst über die Som-

Wer mit offenen Augen nach Mallorca kommt, wird diesen herben, selbstbewussten Charakter schnell erkennen und schätzen lernen.

If you come to Majorca with open eyes, you will quickly spot this dry, self-assured character and learn to appreciate it

emotionally overcharged memories or the idea that, after umpteen summer holidays here, you somehow belong on the island. Majorca is a foreign land – just like anywhere else in the world – best explored with respect and fascination. Without sufficient distance, it's easy to become short-sighted. So, let's consider the facts from the CURVES cockpit: Majorca is the largest of the Balearic Islands in the western Mediterranean. It's around 100 kilometres east to west and 80 kilometres north to south, with a coastline of more than 550 kilometres. The weather is hot and sunny in the summer, mild and occasionally wet in wintertime. Geologically, Majorca and the other Balearic Islands (Menorca, Ibiza, Formentera and more than 140 other uninhabited islands) is on the Iberian Plate. Politically, the Balearics are an autonomous collective within the kingdom of Spain. The Mallorquin dialect spoken on Majorca is a form of Catalan. Having been settled in the Stone Age by peoples from Iberia and modern-day Provence, Majorca managed to remain beneath the radar of great European history for a long time. Notable episodes include a period as part of the Carthaginian Empire and a later switch to the Roman Empire. Influences stem from the Moors and Normans as well as its more recent affiliation with Spain. However, in true island fashion, the dominant culture is Mallorquin – let things come and go but remain firmly the same.

If you come to Majorca with open eyes, you will quickly spot this dry, self-assured character and learn to appreciate it – much like the island's landscape, which is largely rugged and primordial. Spreading inland beyond Palma, S'Arenal and Magaluf is a region called Pla de Mallorca. Baking-hot in summer, these flatlands possess a rustic, agricultural character that is as open and honest as the calloused handshake of an almond farmer. The region of Es Raiguer lies to the northwest and forms the hilly transition

mermonate. Das Llevant-Gebirge im Osten hingegen zeigt sich Besuchern gegenüber ein wenig aufgeschlossener – der ländlichen Gegend im Südosten zeigen wiederum die Touristen häufig eine kalte Schulter. Zu einfach, zu wenig spektakulär.

Für Besucher die das eigentliche Wesen Mallorcas erkunden wollen, entsteht auf einer Rundreise um und über die Insel mit der Zeit ein ganz besonderer Eindruck: Hier kann man sich verlieren. Mallorca ist zu vielfältig, um einfach zu begreifen oder langweilig zu sein. Mallorca hat Gewicht, eine natürliche, erdende Gravitationsenergie, die aus in Jahrhunderten gewachsener Kultur und einer ursprünglichen Natur herrührt. Die an manchen Orten anzutreffende dünne Schicht von künstlicher Tourismus-Parallelwelt wirkt immer so, als sei sie in einem Moment abzuschütteln, die aufgeblasenen Bettenburgen und lärmenden Party-Epizentren ebenso wie das aalglatte Treiben der Vermarktungs-Experten. Luftballon. Nadel. Bamm. Und Mallorca wird immer noch da sein.

COLL DE SÓLLER

Um diese Objektivität zu erreichen, hilft es, sich auf den Weg zu machen. Zu Fuß über die Serra Tramuntana. Mit dem Fahrrad rund um die Insel. Oder mit dem Auto. Einfach losfahren. Die Augen offenhalten. Keine Gefühle jagen, sondern das Leben geschehen lassen. Man mag es – geimpft durch lärmende Last-Minute-Tourismus-Angebote oder Krisen-Portraits – kaum glauben, aber Mallorca ist ziemlich gut in genau einer zeitlosen Disziplin: da sein. Auf der Entdeckungsreise in diese Stille einer selbstbewussten Landschaft trifft man zuerst auf eine Natur, die weit und herb ist, sinnlich und pur. Menschen, die mediterrane Kargheit mögen, sind hier genau richtig. Eine uralte Kulturlandschaft bringt einen dann zu den Menschen, die gefühlt nichts erschüttern kann und unter vorsichtiger Reserviertheit großes Interesse und Wärme verbergen. Und dann sind da noch die Geschichten, die dieses Land erzählt. Episch, tragisch, manchmal sogar komisch. Mit Sonne, Strand und leichtem Leben hat das alles ganz selten etwas zu tun. Sondern im Wesentlichen mit Schönheit. Mallorca, das ist überraschend gut.

to the Serra de Tramuntana with its peaks rising to an altitude of more than 1,000 metres. Wild and solitary, the west of Majorca seems untouched, able to shrug off the tourist influx, even during the summer months. The Llevant mountains in the east, on the other hand, are a little more welcoming to visitors, while tourists tend to turn a cold shoulder to the rural south-eastern region – too simple, not sufficiently spectacular. For visitors wanting to explore the true essence of Majorca, a trip around and across the island gradually reveals a very particular impression – it's quite easy to lose yourself here. Majorca is too diverse a place to grasp easily or to be boring. Majorca has weight – a natural, grounding gravitational energy based on primordial nature and a culture that has grown and developed over centuries. The thin layer of that parallel, artificial world of tourism evident in some places always seems as if it can be shaken off in a matter of moments – the towering hotel complexes and raucous party epicentres along with the slick business conducted by marketing experts. One giant balloon. One tiny needle. BANG. And Majorca will still be there.

In order to achieve this level of objectivity, it helps to travel – on foot across the Serra Tamuntana, around the island on a bicycle or in a car. Just set off and keep your eyes open. Don't go searching for sensations but simply let life happen. It might be hard to believe, immunised as we are by shrieking last-minute tourist deals and crisis portraits, but Majorca is pretty good at one particular, timeless discipline – being. On the voyage of discovery in the silence of a self-assured landscape, what you come upon first is a natural landscape that is expansive and harsh, sensual and pure. People who like Mediterranean sparsity have come to the right place. An ancient cultural landscape then brings you to people who seem unsettled by nothing and who hide great interest and warmth beneath a layer of cautious reserve. And then there are the stories told by this land – epic, tragic and sometimes even funny. It all has very little to do with sun, sea, sand and easy living. Mostly, it's about beauty. Let Majorca surprise you.

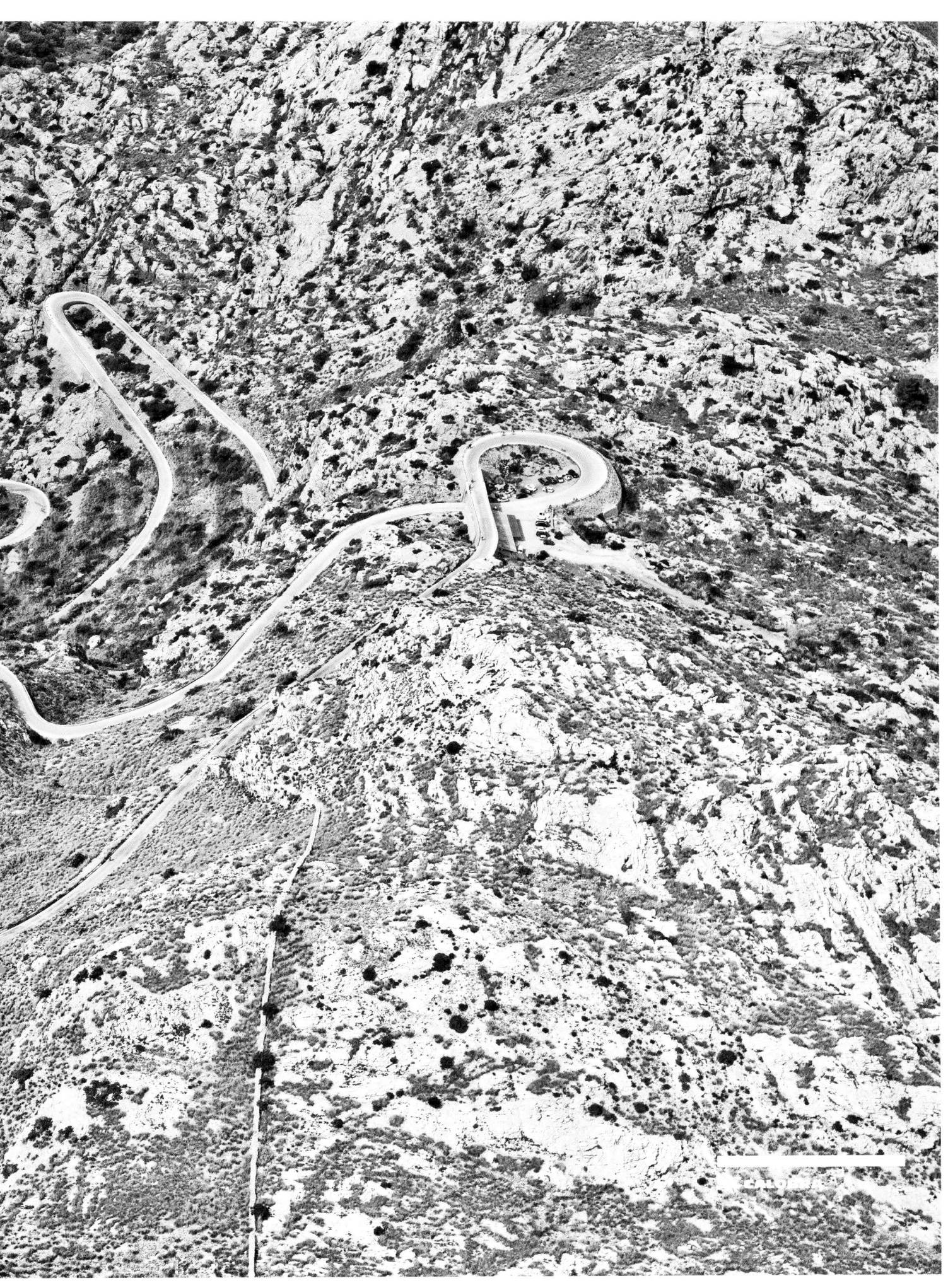

CAP DE FORMENTOR

CAP DE FORMENTOR

SA CALOBRA

CAP DE FORMENTOR

VALLDEMOSSA

ESTELLENCS

COLL DE SÓLLER

SA CALOBRA

CAP DE FORMENTOR

VALLDEMOSSA

PALMA
VALLDEMOSSA

160 KM · 5 STUNDEN // 99 MILES · 5 HOURS

Die Fähre nach Palma de Mallorca geht am Mittag. Barcelona im Rücken, hinaus aufs Mittelmeer. Ein schneeweißer Gigant schiebt sich vibrierend und pulsierend durch das Hafenbecken. Aus den Ramblas der katalanischen Hauptstadt wabern Sound und Geruch einer hyperaktiven Stadt, am Riff des Montjuic kreisen Vogelschwärme und die Bergkette des Tibidabo verschwindet im glasigen Dunst.

—

The ferry to Palma de Mallorca leaves at midday. We set off across the Mediterranean with Barcelona behind us – a snow-white giant pushing its way shuddering and vibrating through the harbour basin. The sounds and smells of a hyperactive city waft from the Catalan capital's famous Las Ramblas. Swarms of birds circle the Montjuic and the Tibadabo Mountains disappear in the haze.

COLL SA CREU

RESTAURANTS

SADRASSANA
PLAÇA DE LA DRASSANA, 15
PALMA
TEL: +34 971 72 85 15
WWW.SADRASSANA.COM

RESTAURANTE LA BÓVEDA
C/ BOTERÍA, 3
PALMA
TEL: +34 971 71 48 63
WWW.RESTAURANTELABOVEDA.COM

HOTELS

HOTEL MAMÁ
PLAÇA DE CORT
PALMA
TEL: +34 871 03 74 37
WWW.HOTELMAMA.ES

HM BALANGUERA
CARRER DE LA BALANGUERA
PALMA
TEL: +34 971 45 61 52
WWW.HMBALANGUERA.COM

Kurs nach Süden, Fahrt aufnehmen, während marodierende Möwen-Gangs an den Schornsteinen der Fähre windsurfen. Sieben Stunden lang Müßiggang an Deck. Sonnenstand beobachten. Spazierrunde Steuerbord rauf, Backbord runter. Mittagessen. Dann: Zeitvertreib. Und gleich nochmal: Zeitvertreib. Die Fähre stampft über das grünschwarze Mittelmeer, eintausendfünfhundert Meter tief, während über uns weiße Kondensstreifen in dieselbe Richtung zielen.

Schon sonderbar, mit dem Schiff nach Mallorca zu fahren, wenn es doch an jedem mittelgroßen Flughafen Europas Billigflüge gibt, die sonnenhungrige Touristen nach Palma de Mallorca schießen. Und dafür kaum mehr Zeit benötigen als es braucht, um einen Actionfilm zu sehen und einen Tomatensaft zu trinken. Aber wir haben besondere Gründe für diese Anreise im Groove des Meeres. Erstens: Atmosphäre. Inseln werden durch das Meer ringsum definiert. Wer hier auf dem Luftweg abkürzt, kennt nicht die ganze Geschichte. Man muss alle Seemeilen abgeritten haben, um wirklich zu verstehen, wo man da eigentlich ist. Mallorca liegt eben nicht eine Stunde hinter dem Gate am Flughafen Manchester oder Düsseldorf, sondern siebeneinhalb Stunden südlich von Barcelona, acht Stunden östlich von Valencia. Eine uralte Balearen-Insel im Wind des Mittelmeers. Geschichtsträchtig. Rau. Vielschichtig. Fremd. Das kann man als einer von täglich 180.000 Sommer-Passagieren im Flughafen-Terminal von Palma de Mallorca irgendwie kaum nachvollziehen. Der zweite Grund für die Anreise ohne den Finger auf der Flugzeug-Fast-Forward-Taste steht im Unterdeck und hat vier Räder. Um Mallorca im Ganzen aufzunehmen, muss man unterwegs sein können, die zerschundenen Mietwagen am Airport-Terminal sind nicht unser Ding.

We set a course south, picking up speed as marauding gangs of seagulls windsurf around the ferry's chimneys. Seven hours wandering around on deck – watching the sun traverse the sky. A stroll one way along the starboard side and back along the port side. Lunch. Then while away the time – before doing it all again from the top. The ferry pounds its way across the green-black waters of the Med, one-thousand-five-hundred metres deep, while, above us, white contrails head in the same direction.

It's a strange experience travelling to Majorca by ship when every mid-sized airport in Europe offers cheap flights sending sun-hungry tourists to Palma de Mallorca – taking little more time than necessary to watch an action movie and drink a tomato juice. But we have a very special reason for this journey in the groove of the sea. Firstly – atmosphere. Islands are defined by the presence of water all around them. If you take the airborne shortcut you know the whole story. You have to have covered all the sea miles to truly understand where you really are. Majorca is not just an hour past the airport gate in Manchester or Düsseldorf, but seven-and-a-half hours south of Barcelona, eight hours east of Valencia. An ancient Balearic island in the Mediterranean wind. Laden with history, raw, multi-facetted, foreign. This is something hard to comprehend as one of the 180,000 summer passengers arriving daily at the airport terminal of Palma de Mallorca. The second reason for travelling without a finger pressed on the aeronautical fast-forward button is below decks and has four wheels. To capture Majorca in its entirety, you have to be able to take to the road, and the scruffy rental cars at the airport terminal just aren't our thing. Nor is the selfie-trip to the coastal viewpoint – when the all-inclusive sunburn is getting too much.

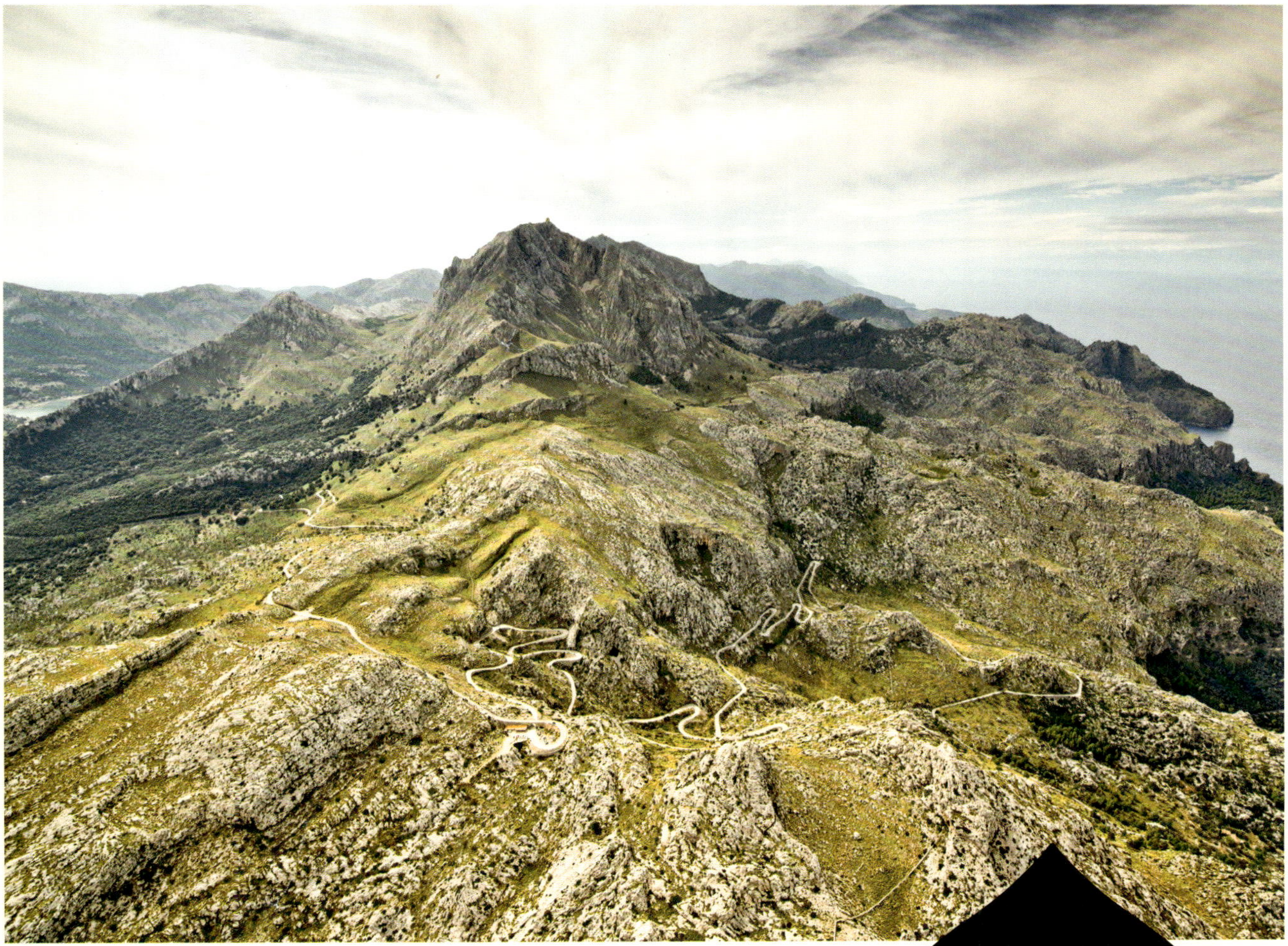

CURVES
MAGAZIN EST. 2011
soulful driving

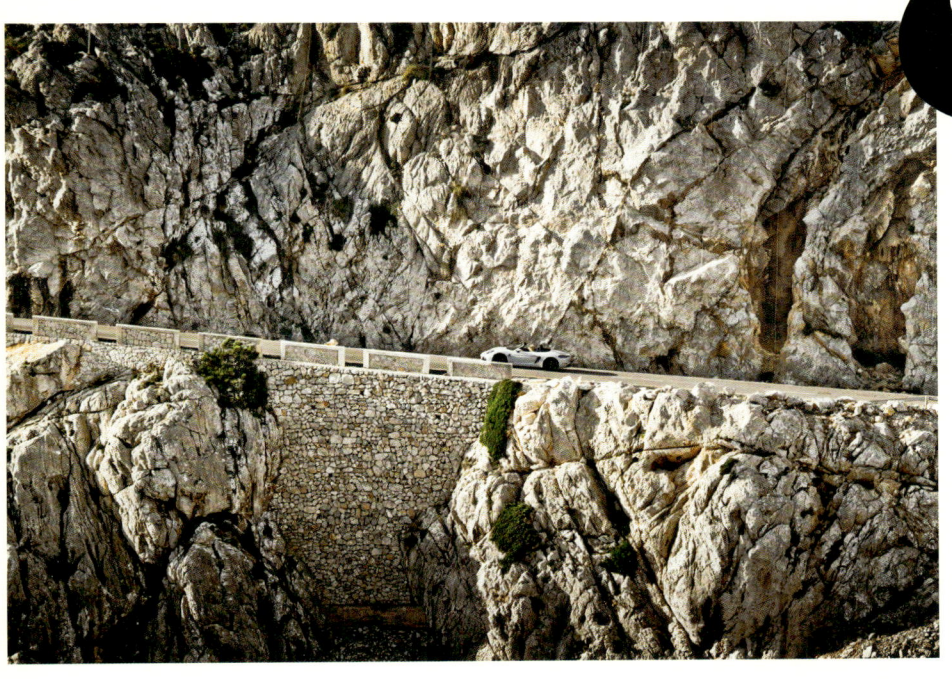

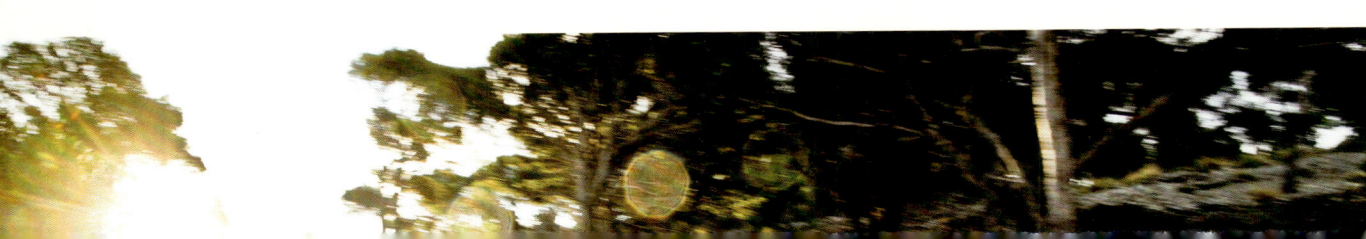

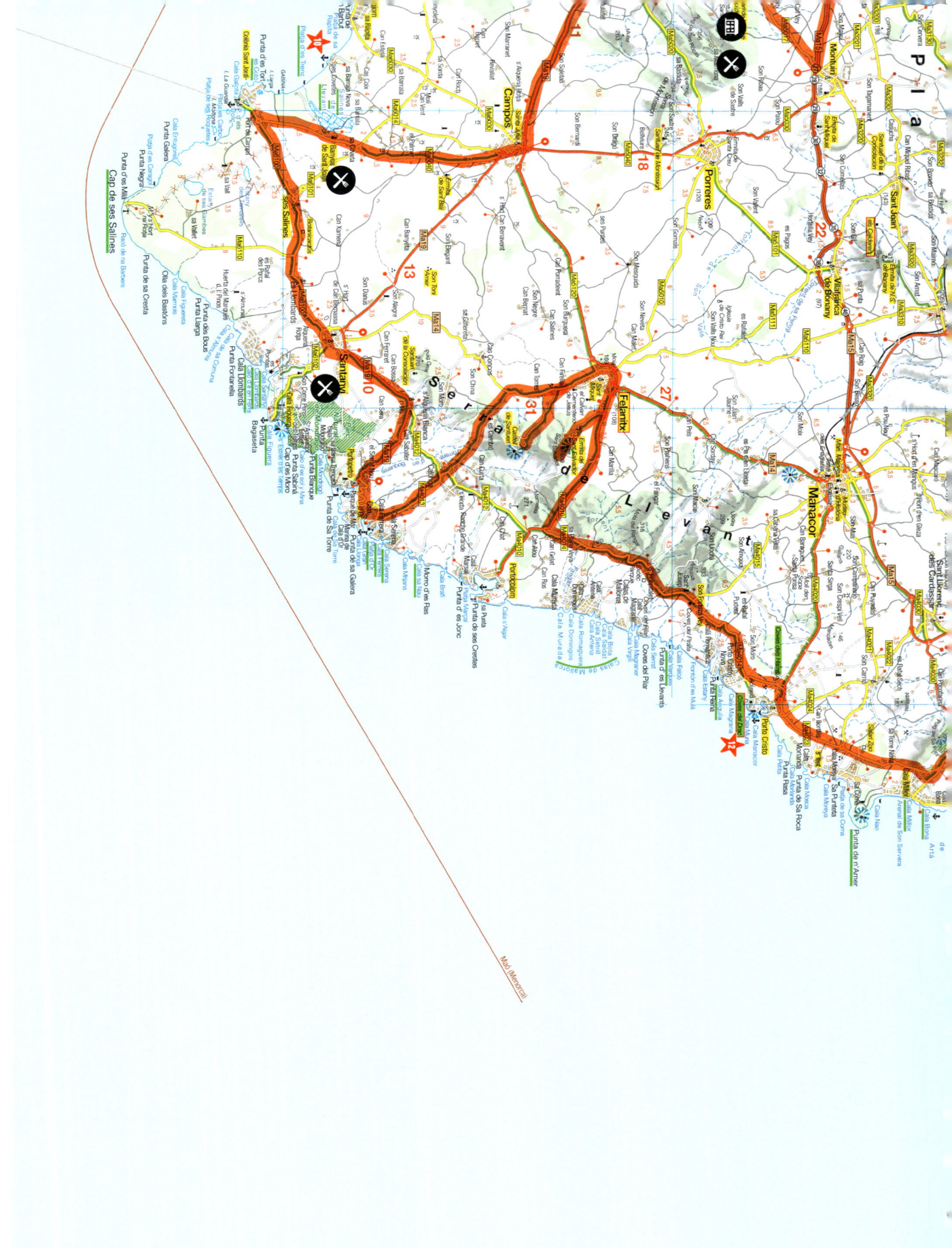

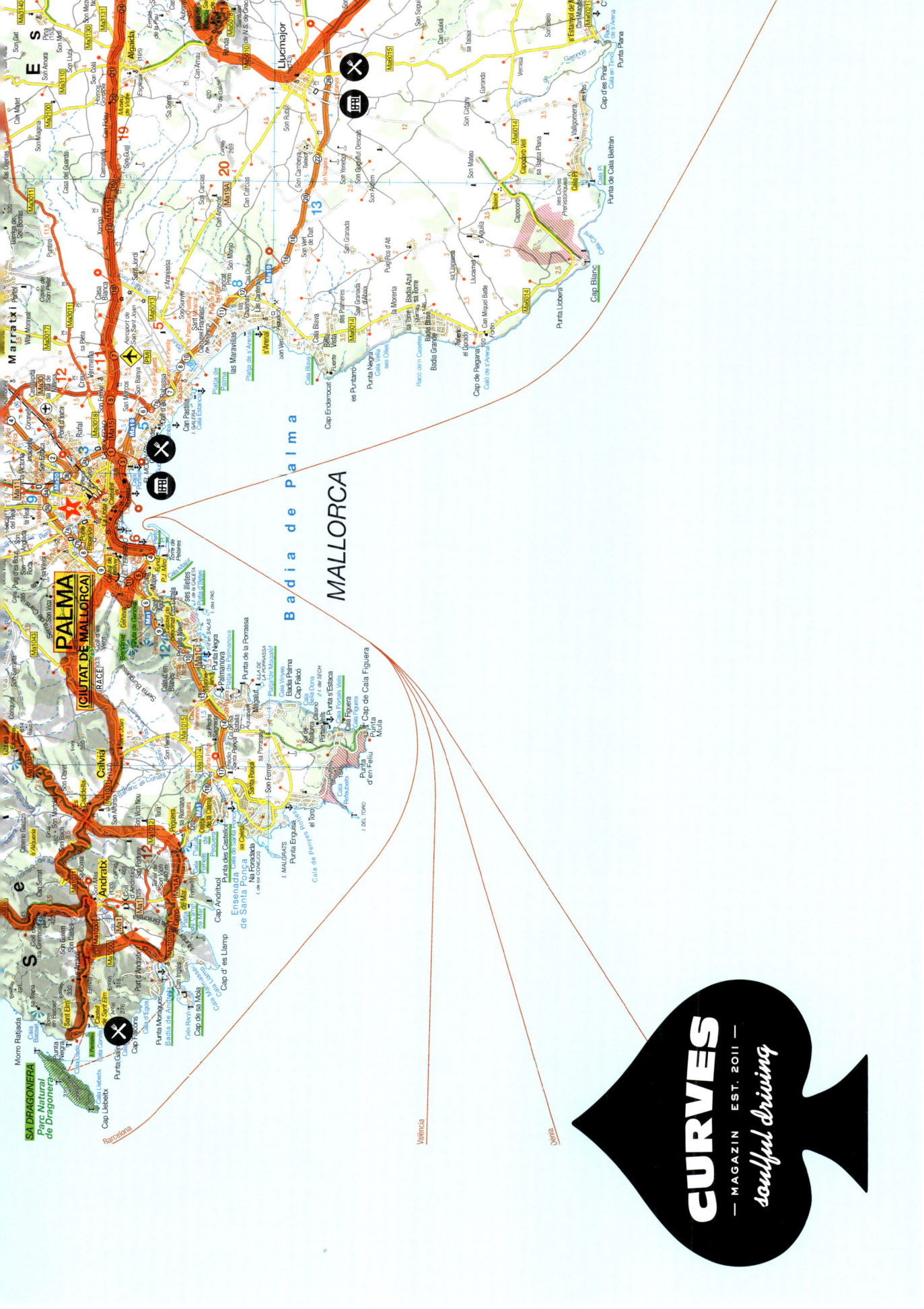

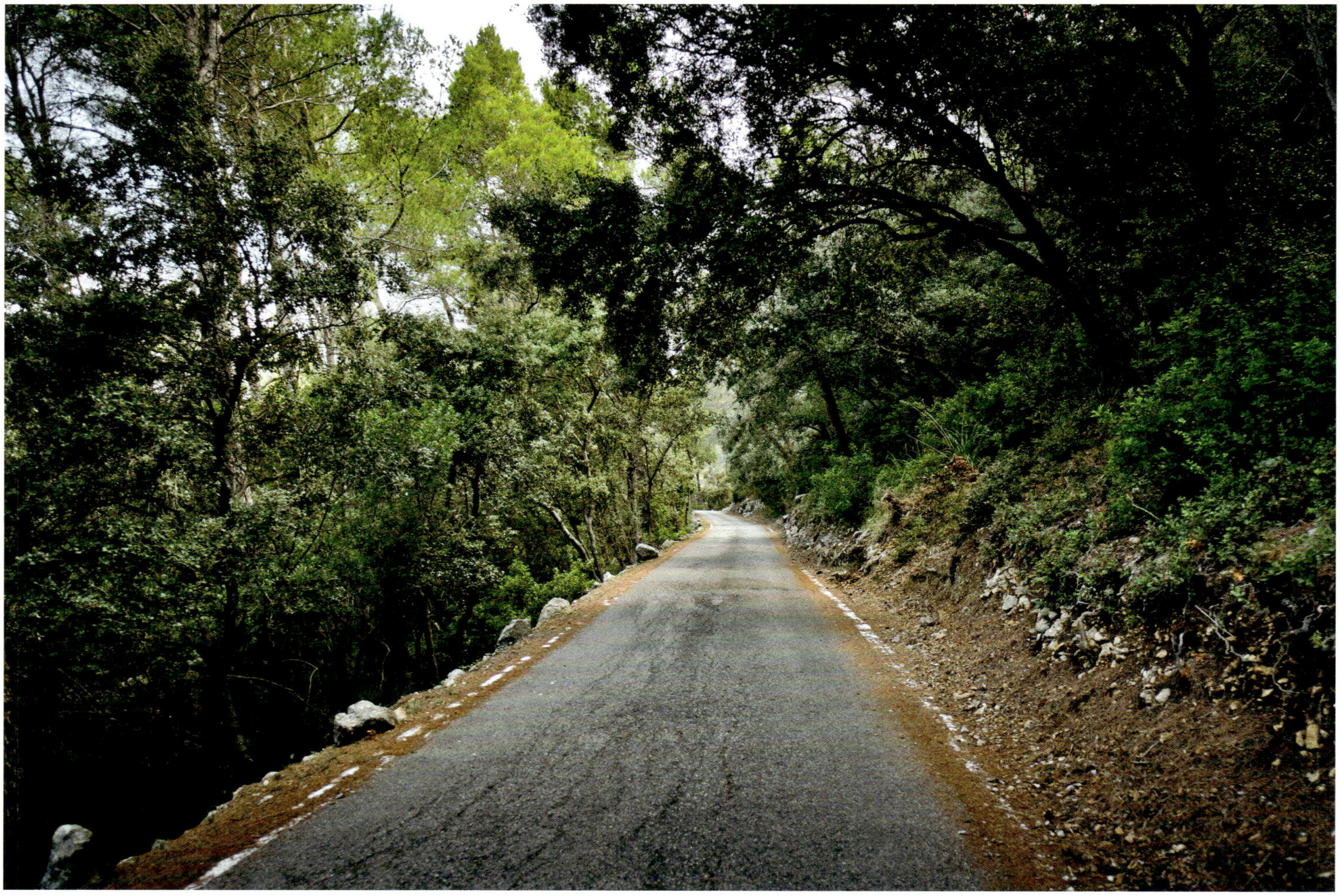

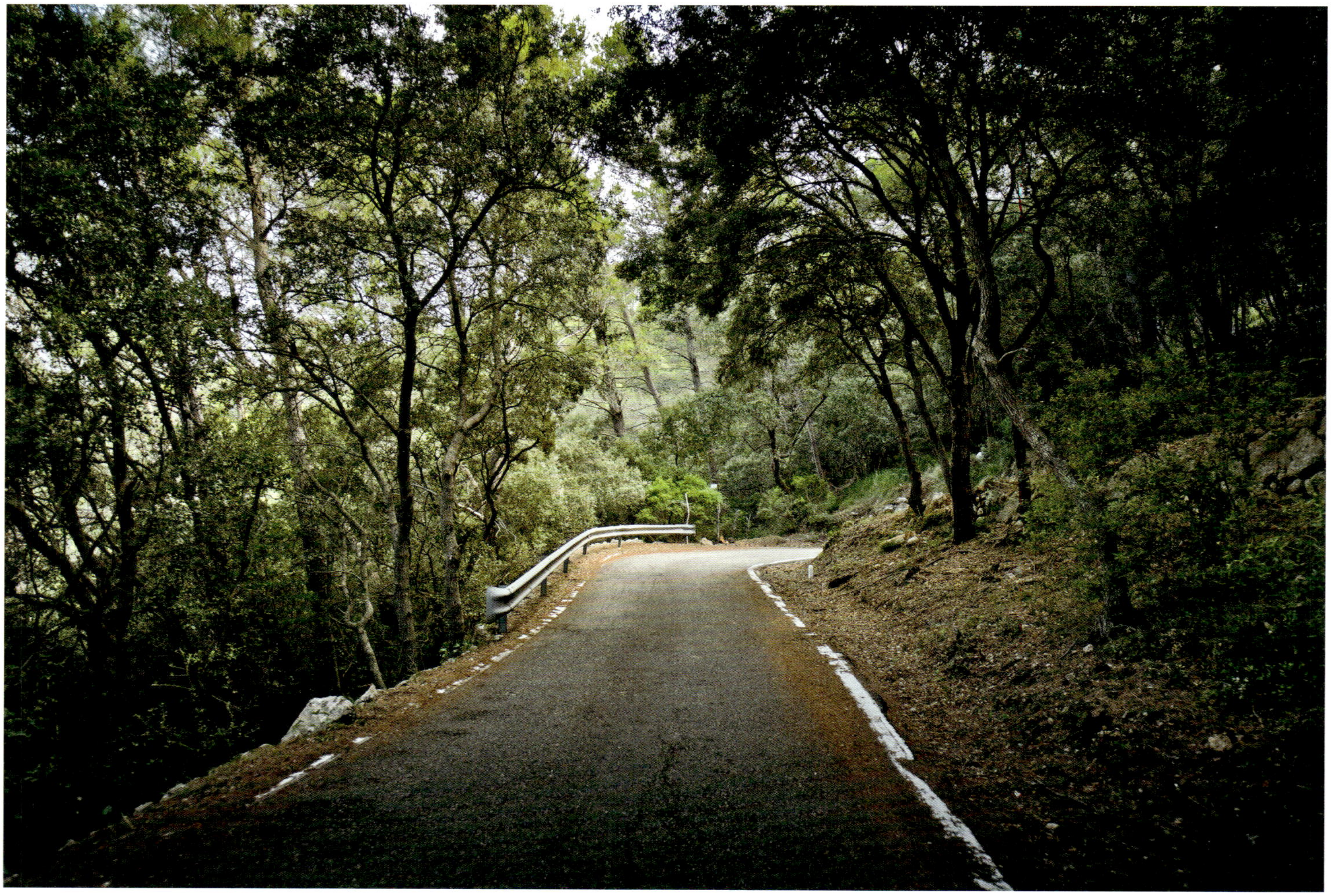

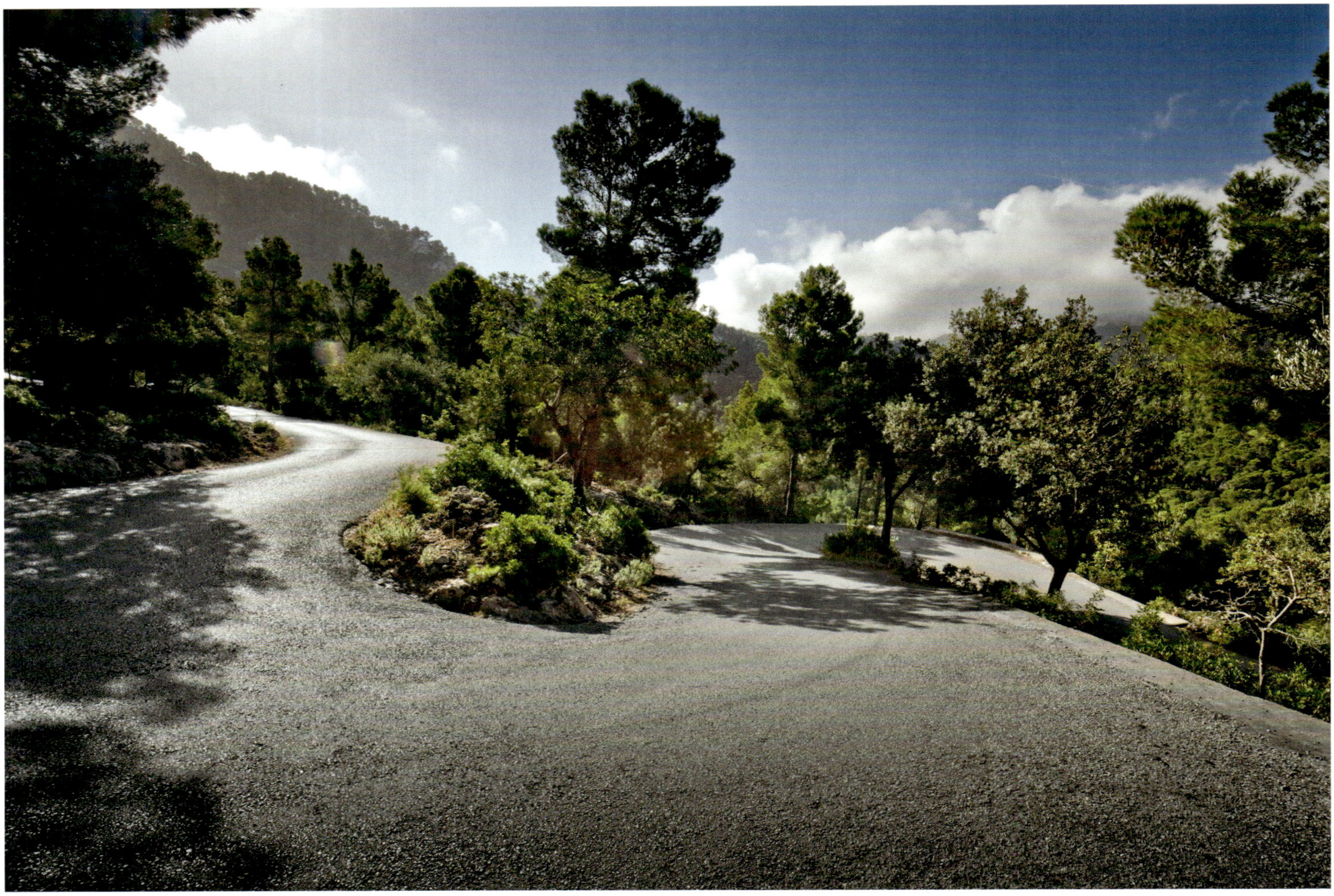
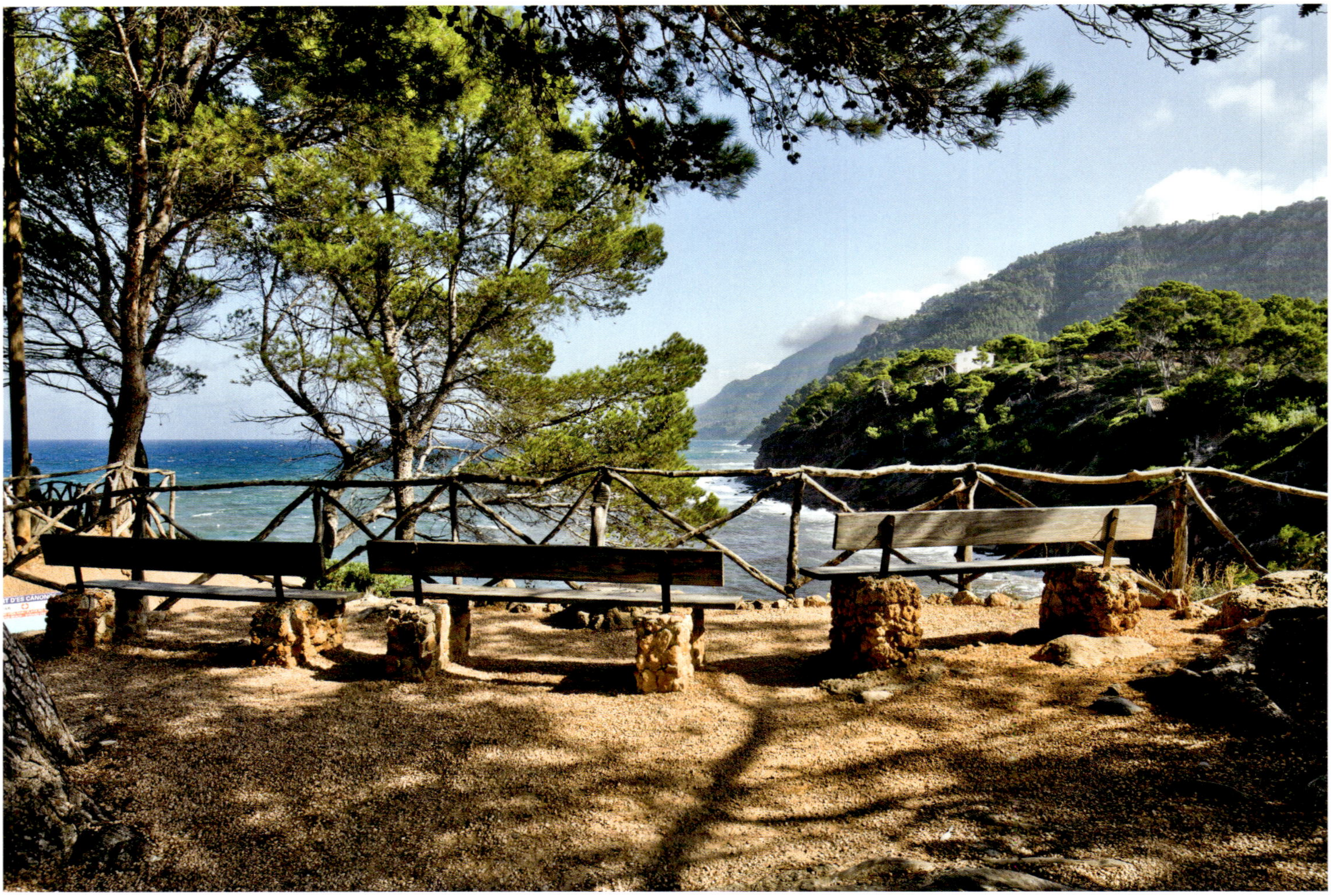

Die Selfie-Fahrt zum Aussichtspunkt am Meer – wenn der All-Inclusive-Sonnenbrand allzu sehr zieht – auch nicht.

Dann, irgendwann, nimmt die Sonne langsam Kurs auf den Horizont im Osten. Voraus erscheint die Silhouette der Insel. Kommt langsam näher, im Wettlauf gegen den Sonnenuntergang. Vorbei an der Westspitze Mallorcas, hinein in die Bucht von Palma. Für einen kurzen Moment sieht es so aus, als ob das Schiff geraden Kurs auf die Stadt nähme, dann dreht es bei und schäumt zu den modernen Beton-Kais des Kreuzfahrt- und Fährterminals. Die Abendsonne hat inzwischen einen magischen Orangeton angenommen, versenkt die Welt in einen psychedelischen Zeitlupe-Rausch, der alle glücklich blinzeln und sich über die Schönheit des Lebens wundern lässt. Im herben Charme des Hafenviertels ist das besonders verstörend: Man sieht selbst den tätowierten und gegerbten Auswinkern an, wie sie gänsehäutig und in andächtiger Stille ein Auto nach dem anderen aus dem Bauch der Fähre auf den Kai entlassen.

Wir steuern in der beginnenden Dämmerung nach Osten und stoppen nach wenigen hundert Metern vor der mächtigen Bischofskirche von Palma. Die Kathedrale La Seu mit ihren ausgestellten Stützpfeilern ähnelt einer massigen Spinne, im Dunkeln beleuchtet wird sie zum Exoskelett einer außerirdischen Lebensform. Gestrandet im frühen Mittelalter auf dem Fundament einer maurischen Moschee, schlafend seit über siebenhundert Jahren. Rund um den steinernen Giganten lärmt das Leben der mallorquinischen Hauptstadt. Musik, Hupen, Gelächter – wie wir nun aber so ans Auto gelehnt zum riesigen Schatten von La Seu hinüberschauen, scheint die Kirche beinahe zu atmen. Endlos ruhig, unbeeindruckt, ewig. Vom Hafen her zieht der mürbe Duft des Meeres, der Himmel glimmt in tiefblauem Schwarz und plötzlich tritt alles

Then, eventually, the sun slowly heads for the eastern horizon as the island's silhouette emerges in the distance ahead. It draws gradually nearer – in a race against the sunset. We pass the western tip of Majorca and head into the Bay of Palma. For a brief moment, it seems as if the ship is heading straight for the city. Then it heaves to and foams its way alongside the modern concrete quays of the cruise-ship and ferry terminal. Meanwhile, the evening sun has taken on a magical orange hue, bathing the world in a psychedelic slow-mo fuzz that makes everyone blink happily and marvel at the beauty of life. This is particularly unsettling in the austere charm of the harbour district – even the tattooed, weather-beaten ferrymen are transfixed in awestruck silence as they wave one car after another out of the belly of the ferry and onto the quayside.

We turn east in the early twilight and stop after a few hundred metres in front of Palma's magnificent La Seu Cathedral – its exposed supporting pillars giving it the appearance of an enormous spider. Illuminated against the night sky, it becomes the exoskeleton of an alien lifeform – stranded in the early Middle Ages on the foundations of a Moorish mosque, slumbering for more than seven hundred years. The daily hubbub of life in the Majorcan capital continues unabated around the stone colossus. Music, horns, laughter – as we stand leaning against the car gazing at La Seu's enormous shadow, the cathedral almost seems to be breathing. Infinitely calm, unimpressed, eternal. The mellow scent of the sea drifts up from the harbour, while the sky smoulders to a deep-blue black and suddenly everything fades into the distance. We're completely alone here in this moment. Nobody at home will believe that our trip around Majorca began like this. The gaudy, cliched images of the pulsating nightlife are overpowering, but the reality today is very

HELI

ROTORFLUG HELICOPTERS SL
AERÓDROMO DE SON BONET
07141 PALMA DE MALLORCA
WWW.ROTORFLUG.COM/DE/
STANDORTE/PALMA-DE-MALLORCA

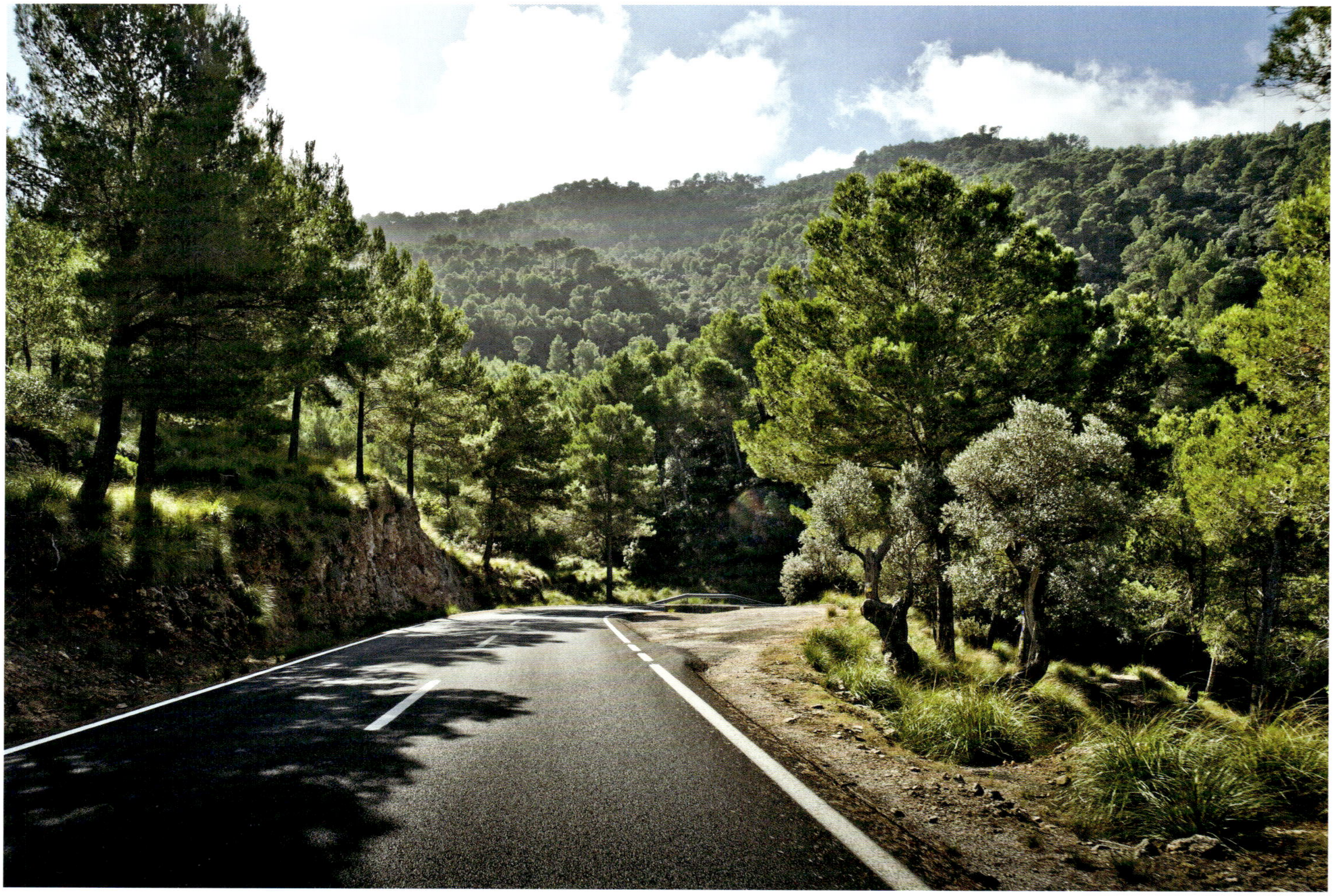

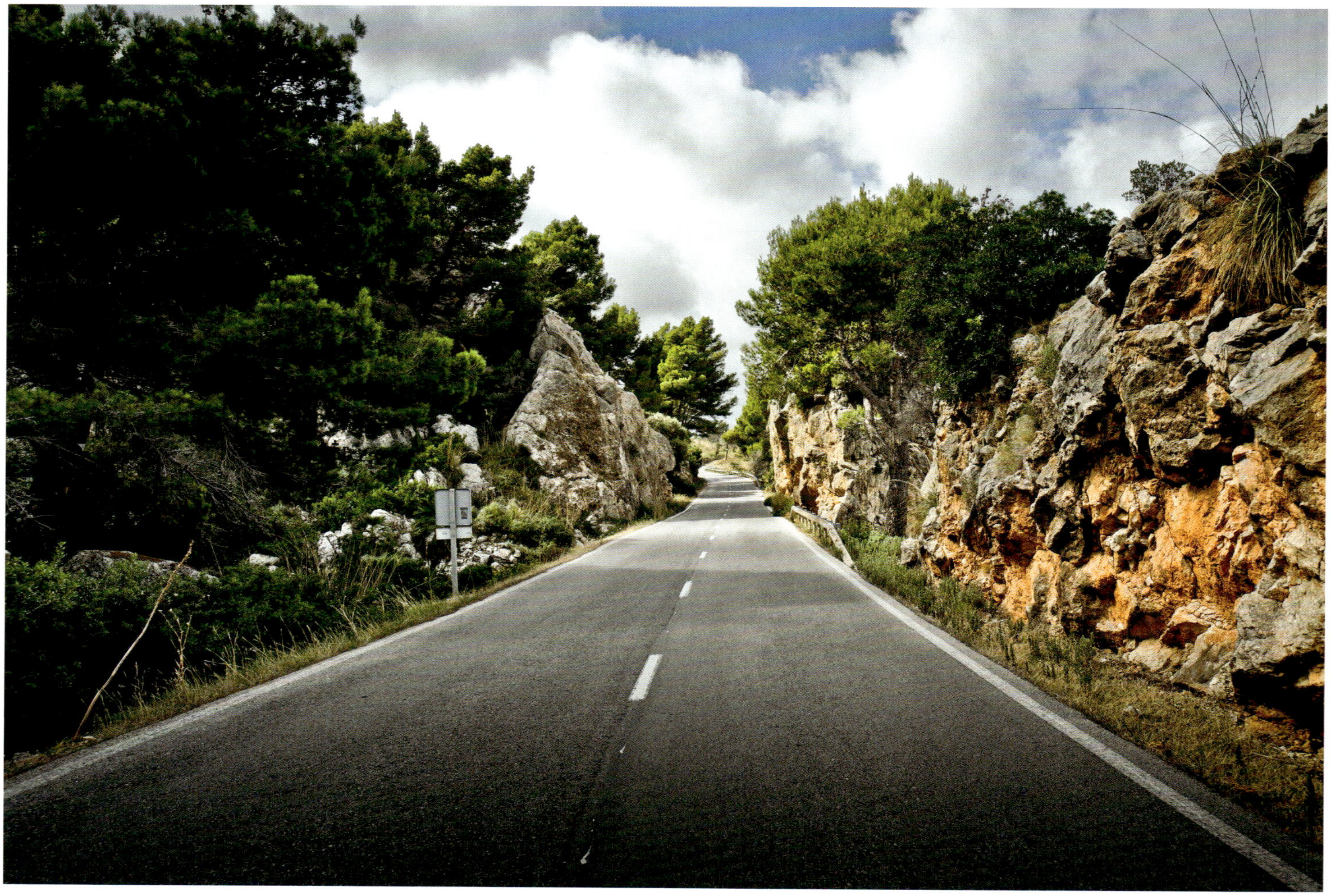

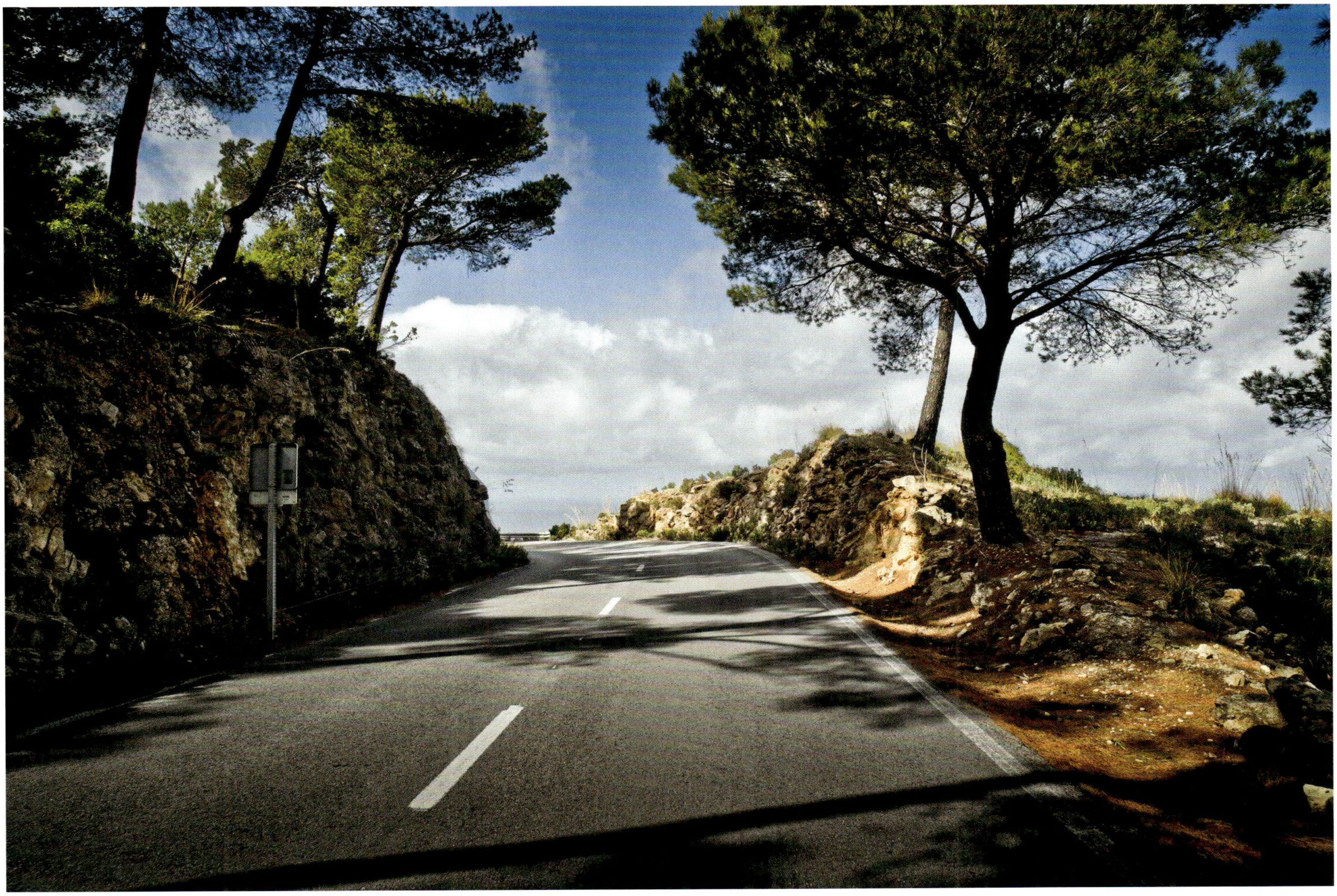

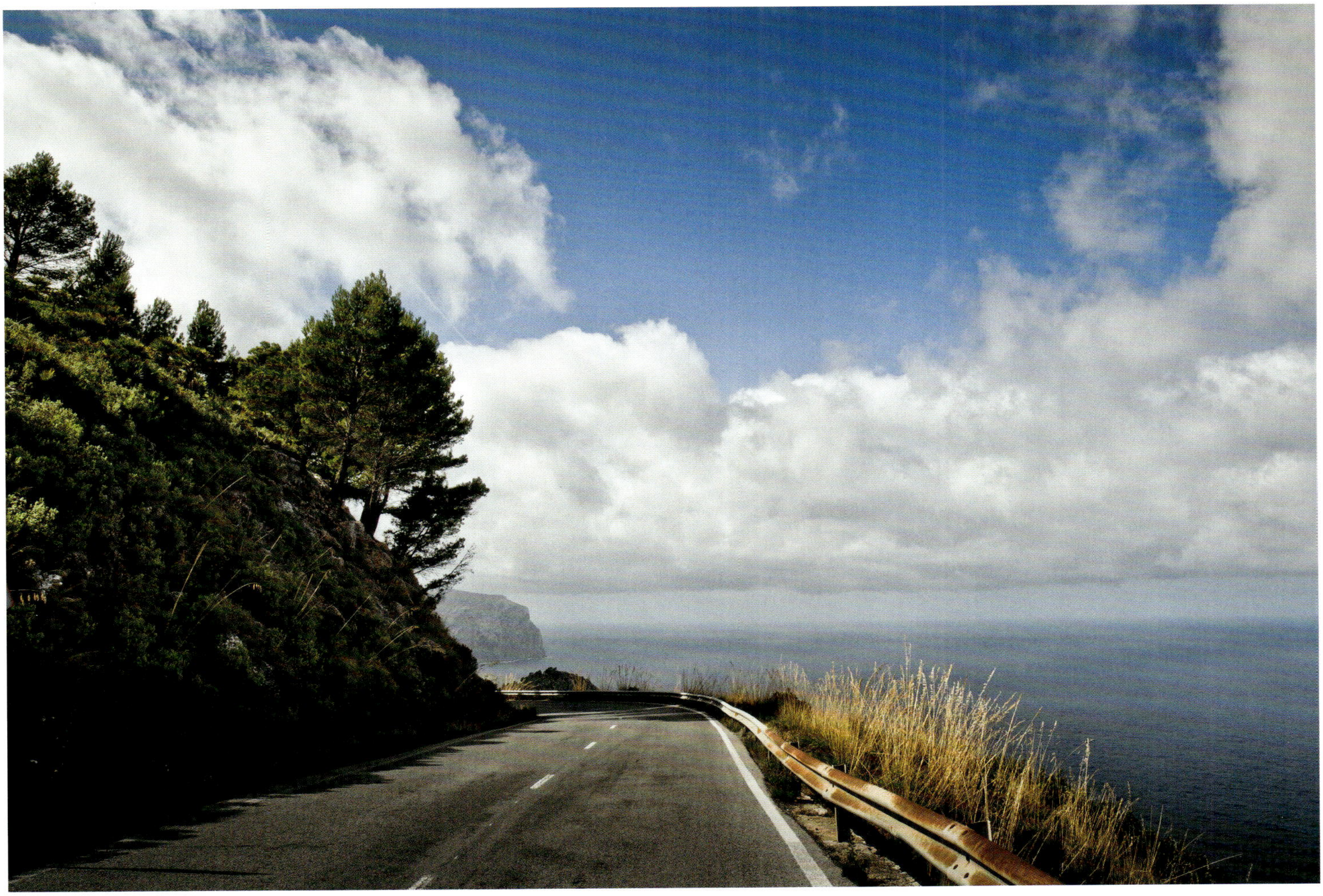

ESTELLENCS

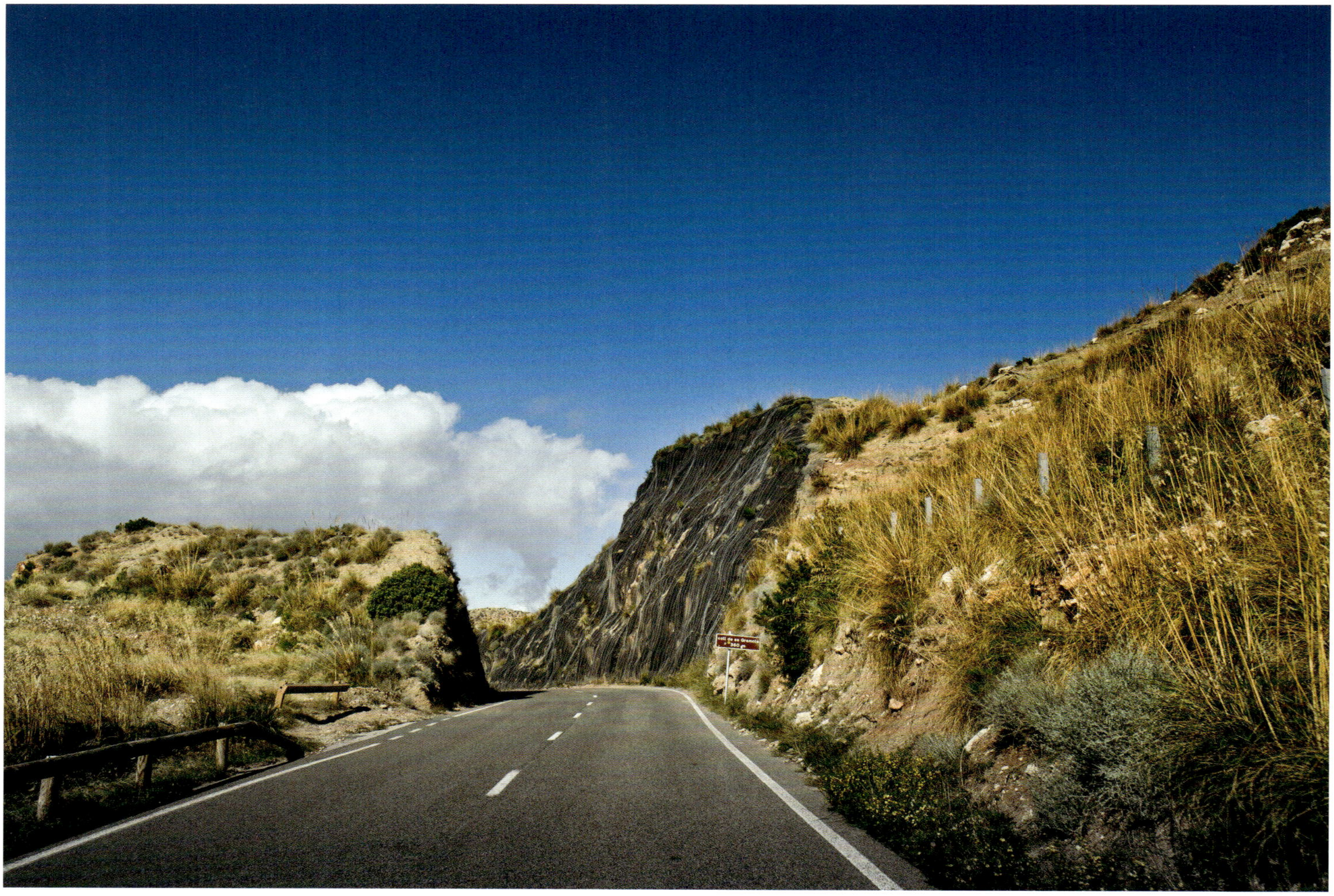

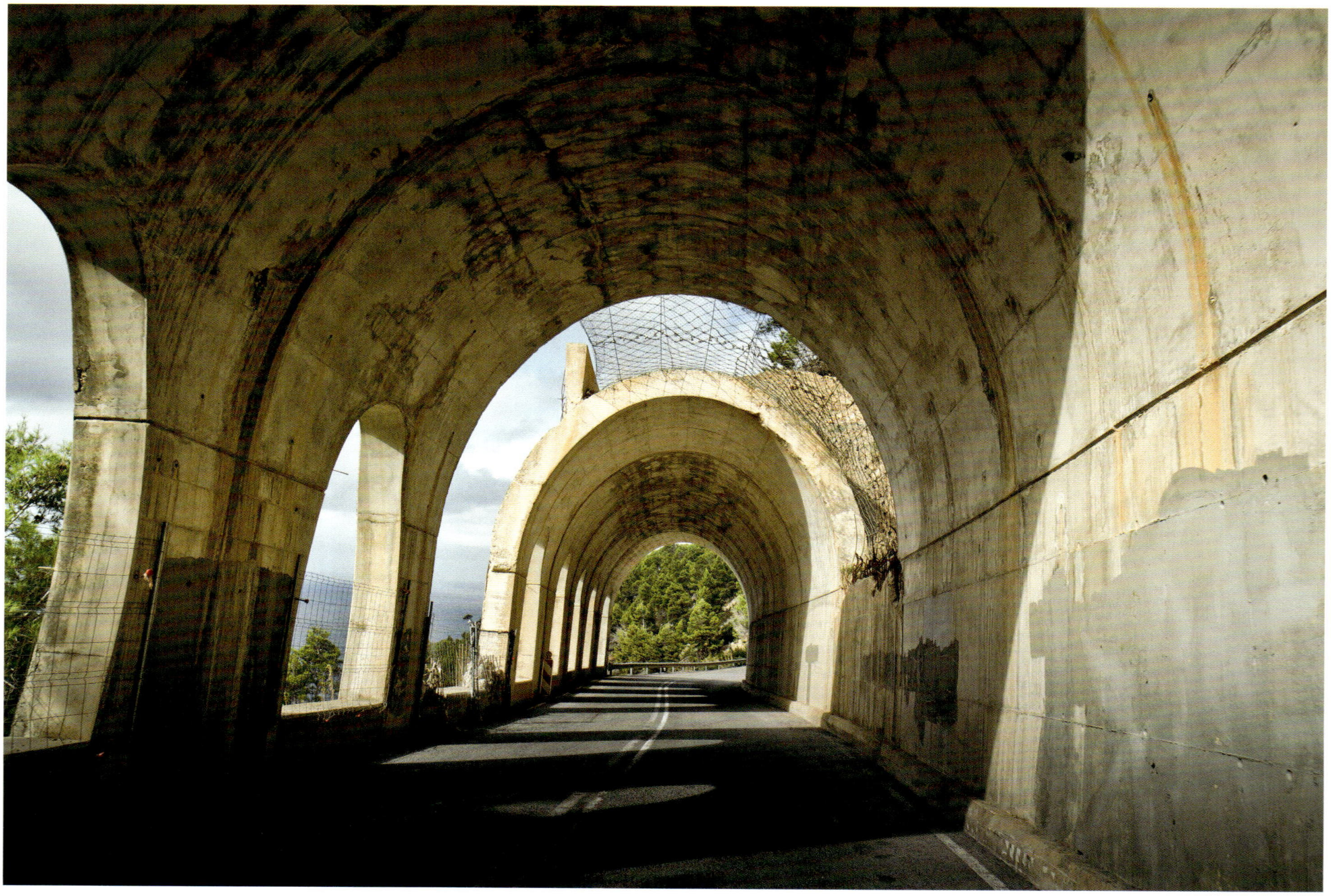

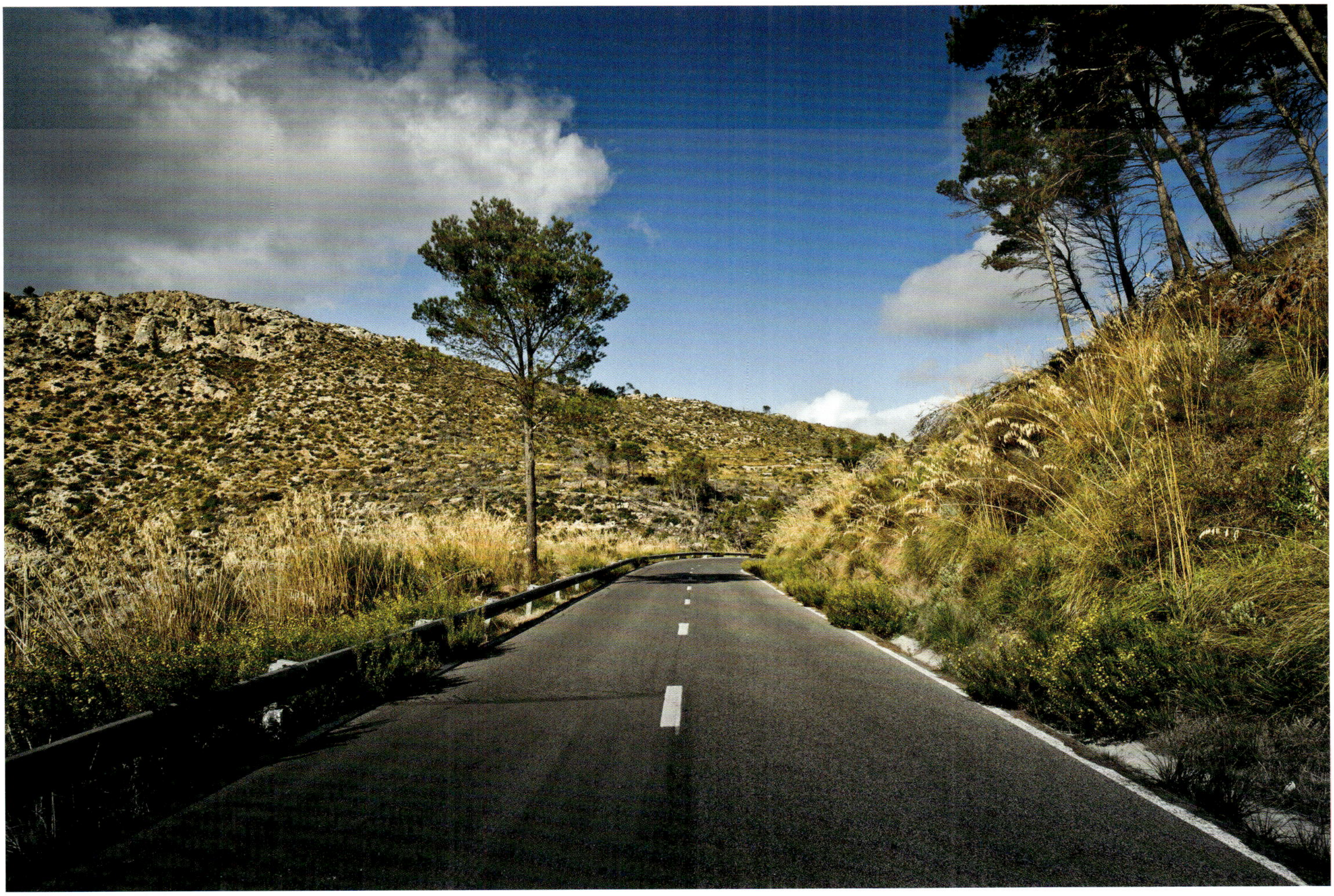

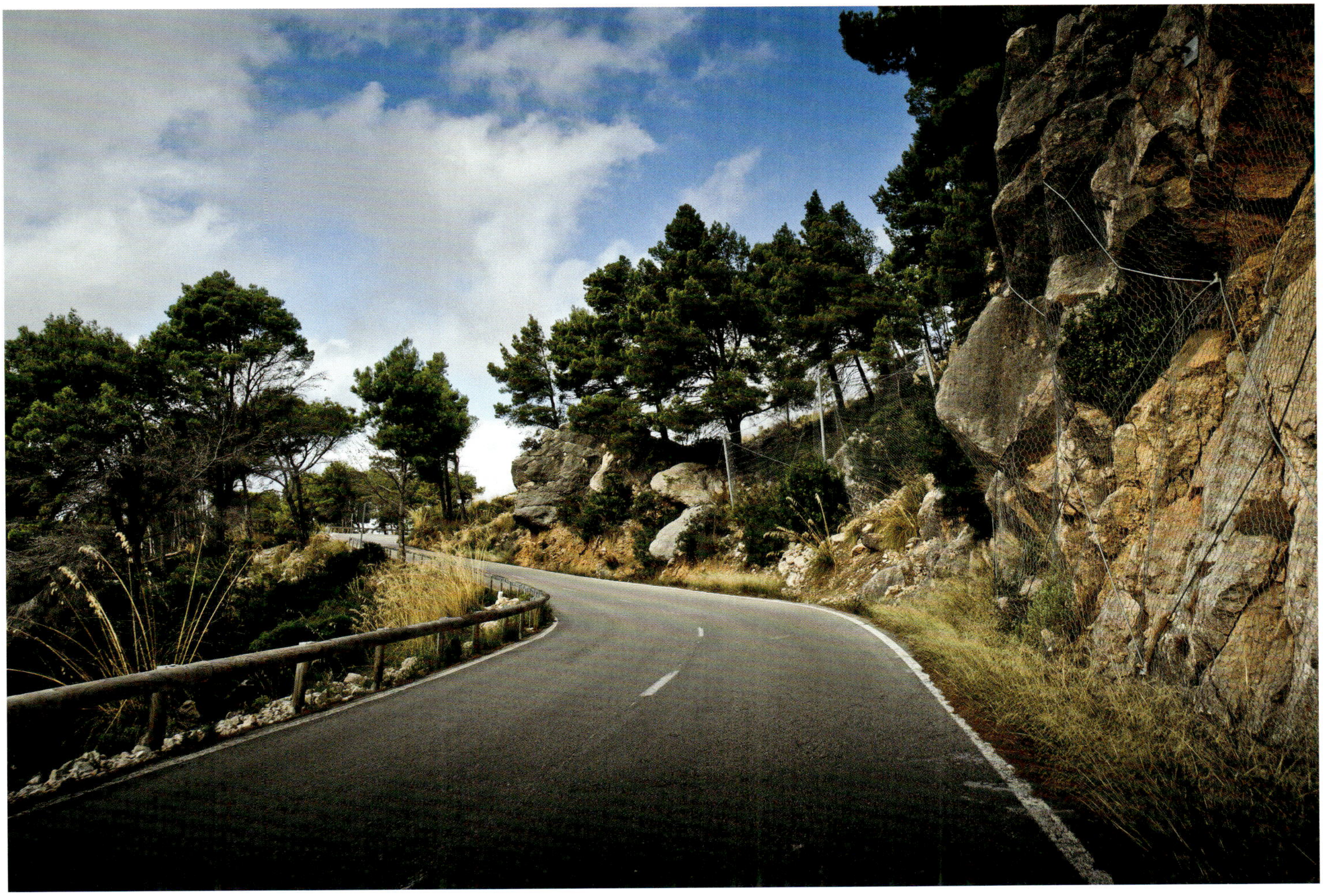

ESTELLENCS

ESTELLENCS

zurück. Wir sind ganz allein hier, in diesem Moment. Zu Hause wird uns niemand glauben, dass unsere Reise rund um Mallorca so begonnen haben soll. Die grellen Klischee-Bilder der Partymeilen sind übermächtig. Aber die Realität ist heute ganz anders. Diese Nacht gehört uns und einem Himmel voller Sterne.

Am nächsten Morgen ist Palma schon wieder laut, voll und aufgedreht, wir kurven durch die Stadt nach Westen. Vorbei an der Abtei Sant Francesc und der alten Festungsanlage Es Baluard. Kurzer Blick hinauf zum Castell de Bellver, der Hügelburg über der Bucht, und dann am Meer entlang in Richtung Südwest. Die Hauptstadt mit ihren Randgebieten läuft nur langsam aus: Wohngebiete, Hotelanlagen und die typischen Attraktionen einer Touristenstadt am Meer reihen sich aneinander. Freizeit- und Themenparks, Erlebnisbäder und Golfplätze drängen sich auf den ersten Kilometern zwischen Ausfallstraße und Küste, den Besuch im benachbarten Santa Ponça sparen wir uns. Soll schön sein dort, aber wir haben Fahrt aufgenommen. Wir sind nicht hier, um anzukommen, haben kein Handtuch auf irgendeine Sonnenliege drapiert, um einen Platz zu reservieren. Aktueller Status: nicht zu stoppen. Und die nur vier Kilometer lange, aber unglaublich vielversprechende Kurvenstrecke zwischen Es Camp de Mar und Port d'Andratx verschafft uns endlich ein Ventil für den inneren Bewegungsdrang, der uns auf die Insel geführt hat. Nach den letzten Häusern geht es in saftigen Schwüngen durch lichten Pinienwald in die Hügel. Wir surfen die Kurven wie Helden – dann ist schon wieder alles zu Ende. Der Hafen von Port d'Andratx sieht herrlich aus, aber wir lassen ihn links liegen, rollen weiter in Richtung S'Arraco und dann runter nach Sant Elm. Weitere knapp 10 Kilometer für den inneren Fahrerlebnis-Speicher,

different altogether. This night belongs to us and a sky full of stars. The next morning, Palma is loud, packed and totally buzzing as we wind our way westwards through the city, past the Franciscan Monastery and the old Es Baluard Fortress. We cast a brief glance up to the Castell de Bellver, the castle on the hill overlooking the bay, before heading southwest along the coast. The capital city and its outlying areas take some time to dissipate – residential neighbourhoods, hotel complexes and the typical attractions of a tourist beach city stand cheek-by-jowl. For the first few kilometres, leisure facilities and theme parks, water attractions and golf courses jostle for position between the ring road and the coast. We spare ourselves a visit to neighbouring Santa Ponça. We've been told it's lovely, but we've picked up momentum and want to keep going. We're not here to arrive anywhere, we haven't draped towels on sun loungers to reserve our spot. Our current status is not to stop. And the winding road between Es Camp de Mar and Port d'Andratx, although only four kilometres long, is extremely inviting and finally provides us with a relief valve for the inner urge to move that led us to the island in the first place. Once we leave the last buildings behind us, the route sweeps gently into the hills through sparse pine forest. We surf the curves like heroes – but it's over far too soon. The harbour area of Port d'Andratx looks gorgeous but we roll on by, heading for S'Arraco and then down to Sant Elm. Another ten kilometres or so for our internal memory bank of driving experiences slowly filling with the scent of pine resin and dusky forest, sunshine and the wind in our hair.

It keeps us going until we stop for a short break in Sant Elm and discuss whether the boat trip to the nearby island of Sa Dragonera

RESTAURANTS

RESTAURANTE 1661
CUINA DE BANYALBUFAR
CALLE BARONIA 1-3
07191 BAÑALBUFAR
TEL: +34 971 61 82 45

ES MOLI SANT ELM
PLAZA DE MOSSEN SEBASTIA GRAU
07159 SANT ELM
TEL: +34 971 23 92 02
WWW.RESTAURANTESMOLI.COM

RESTAURANTE MONTIMAR
PLAZA CONSTITUCIÓ 7
07192 ESTELLENCS
TEL: +34 971 61 85 76
WWW.RESTAURANTELABOVEDA.COM

PORT DE VALLDEMOSSA

der sich langsam mit dem Duft von Pinien-
harz und staubigem Wald, Sonnenstrahlen
und Fahrtwind füllt.

Das reicht in Sant Elm wenigstens für einen kleinen Stopp und die Diskussion, ob
denn die Bootsfahrt zur nahegelegenen
Insel Sa Dragonera ebenfalls ins Programm
unserer Mallorca-Rundfahrt gehören müsste. Der Vorschlag wird aber schnell ver-
worfen und auf „später vielleicht" verscho-
ben. Denn es gibt hier unten am Westzipfel
der Insel noch viel mehr zu entdecke Hoch
nach Andratx, dann Richtung Norden,
Richtung Estellencs. Schwindlig fahren? –
Das ist hier problemlos möglich. Und die
Zivilisation schlagartig Geschichte. Die
Serra de Tramuntana hat uns. Felsentäler
die ins Gebirge streben, schmale Straßen-
Durchlässe zwischen Felstürmen, dann die
azurblaue Weite des Mittelmeers tief unten. Und eine Straße, die sich vollkommen
austobt, um alle Achsen Ekstase, gefühl-
voll und mächtig: Kurven in allen Radien,
aufmachend und zuziehend, Kuppen und
Senken. Am Lenkrad wirst du da ganz still
und konzentriert und glücklich. Es gibt viel
zu tun. Und viel zu sehen. Keine 100 Meter
gleichen denen davor, aber diese Berge sind
so schön, dass man nach beinahe jeder
Kehre wieder die Kamera auspacken möchte um einen epischen Ansel-Adams-Schuss
zu jagen. Irgendwann rollen wir hoch oben
über dem Meer aus, müssen an die eingeöl-
ten Menschenheringe unten am Sangria-
Beach denken und empfinden großes Mit-
leid. Schade, dass die eigentlich noch nie
auf Mallorca waren. Sondern immer nur
an diesem Strand direkt hinter dem Gate
an einem Flughafen 2000 Kilometer weiter nördlich. Ein kleiner Disput folgt direkt
danach: Ob es denn jetzt nicht noch besser
wäre, wenn man diese Straße am Rand der
Insel mit dem Fahrrad absolvieren könnte? Wadenschmalz statt Pferdestärken, ein-
tauchen in die vielen Momente der Landschaft statt die Landschaft zum vielfältigen

is another must-do on the itinerary of our
journey around Majorca. However, the sug-
gestion is quickly dismissed and filed in the
"maybe later" folder as there is plenty more
to discover down here at the island's west-
ernmost tip. We drive up to Andratx then
head north towards Estellencs. We could
easily drive ourselves dizzy here. And suddenly, civilisation is history. The Serra de
Tramuntana has us in its grip – rocky gorg-
es reaching deep into the mountains, narrow passes between towering stone edifices
then the azure-blue expanse of the Mediterranean far below. And a road that runs
absolute riot, delivering ecstasy at all four
wheels – sensitive and mighty. Curves in
all radii – opening up and tightening – ri-
ses and dips. At the wheel, you become totally silent and focused – and happy. There's
lots to do. And lots to see. No 100 metres
is the same as the last, but these mountains are so beautiful that you want to take
your camera out at virtually every turn in
the search for an epic Ansel Adams shot.
At some point, we emerge at the top, high
above the sea and find ourselves pitying the
oiled human herrings down below on Sangria Beach. It's such a shame that they have
never actually been to Majorca but only
ever to that beach right next to the gate of
an airport 2000 kilometres further north.
A brief dispute ensues – wouldn't it be better to travel this road around the edge of the
island on a bicycle? Calf ointment instead
of horsepower, deep-diving into the myr-
iad moments of this landscape instead of
transforming the landscape into a single
multi-faceted moment? Part of us says yes,
that would be perfect. But the other half
wants to press onward right now to the terraced slopes of Banyalbufar, stopping off at
Torre de ses Ànimes then up into the mountains to Galilea at the foot of the Galatzó,
on to Es Capdellà, back to Andratx and then
do the whole thing again until we find ourselves back in Banyalbufar. We won't stop
today until we reach Valldemossa and that

HOTELS

HOTEL CA'S PAPÀ
C/ JOVELLANOS, 8
07170 VALLDEMOSSA
TEL: +34 971 61 28 08
WWW.HOTELCASPAPA.COM

Und jetzt: vollstrecken. Zurück in den Kurven-Orbit. Zurück in die Welt des griffigen Asphalts, der Steinmauern am Straßenrand, der wilden Täler, schattigen Serpentinen und sonnigen Geraden. Diese Berge geben uns den Rest, gleich am ersten Tag unserer Mallorca-Rundfahrt: Flow-Glück

But now, let's get on with it – back into curve orbit. Back into the world of grippy asphalt, stone walls lining the roads, rugged valleys, shady serpentines and sunny straights. These mountains give us their all, on the very first day of our Majorca tour – flow joy.

Moment zu verwandeln? – Ja, das wär's, meint unsere eine Hälfte, aber die andere will jetzt und sofort weiter bis zu den Terrassenhängen von Banyalbufar, Zwischenstopp am Torre de ses Ànimes, dann hoch in die Berge, nach Galilea am Fuß des Galatzó, weiter nach Es Capdellà und dann in Andratx die ganze Runde noch einmal von vorn bis wir wieder in Banyalbufar angekommen sind. Erst in Valldemossa wäre dann für heute Schluss, das schaffst du auf diesem Terrain unmöglich mit dem Rad. Über 100 Kilometer Kurventanz in den Bergen, verlockende Selbstauslöschung.

Unser Auto steht ein paar Meter weit entfernt, duftet nach warmem Öl und heißen Bremsen, das gibt den Ausschlag: Heute ist ein Tag für Oktanschädel. Fahrtwind auf Fast Forward. Aber wir werden ganz bestimmt mit der Rennmaschine zurück sein, an anderen Tagen. Allein mit dem Gedanken schält sich schon ein wohliger Wadenkrampf heraus. Und jetzt: vollstrecken. Zurück in den Kurven-Orbit. Zurück in die Welt des griffigen Asphalts, der Steinmauern am Straßenrand, der wilden Täler, schattigen Serpentinen und sonnigen Geraden. Diese Berge geben uns den Rest, gleich am ersten Tag unserer Mallorca-Rundfahrt: Flow-Glück. Als wir am Abend in Valldemossa einlaufen, sind wir in einer anderen Welt angelangt. Einem Reich hinter den Bergen. Die Sonne streicht übers Meer und tüncht die Stadt an den Hängen in warmen Goldton. Hätten wir je an Mallorca gezweifelt– spätestens jetzt wäre das passé.

would be impossible to achieve on this terrain with a bicycle. Waltzing 100 kilometres through the mountains – tantalising self-obliteration.

Our car stands a few metres away smelling of warm oil and hot brakes. It takes the decision for us – today is a day for petrolheads, foot down on fast forward. But we will definitely return on other days with the racing bikes. Just the thought of it sends blissful cramping sensations shuddering through our calves. But now, let's get on with it – back into curve orbit. Back into the world of grippy asphalt, stone walls lining the roads, rugged valleys, shady serpentines and sunny straights. These mountains give us their all, on the very first day of our Majorca tour – flow joy. When we arrive in Valldemossa that evening, we enter a different world – a land beyond the mountains. The sun washes over the sea and paints the town on the slopes in a warm golden glow. If we had ever had any doubts about Majorca they would have completely evaporated by now.

PALMA VALLDEMOSSA

Die erste Etappe auf unserer Mallorca-Runde widmet sich dem sonnigen Südwesten der Insel und der Serra de Tramuntana. Wir starten in der ebenso turbulenten wie geschichtsträchtigen Hauptstadt Palma de Mallorca, streifen dann die Küste entlang nach Südwesten und statten den bildschönen Fischerdörfern Sant Elm und Port d'Andratx einen Besuch ab. Von hier geht es zuerst ins Landesinnere, dann über die Berge der Tramuntana an die Westküste. Wir folgen der Küstenlinie bis Banyalbufar und erforschen nun den Gebirgszug auf einem Loop im Inneren zurück bis Andratx. Die Runde wird bei Banyalbufar wieder abgeschlossen, auf den nun folgenden Kilometern bis Valldemossa lassen wir die erste Tagesetappe ausklingen

—

The first stage of our journey around Majorca is dedicated to the sunny southwest of the island and the Serra de Tramuntana. We start in the capital, Palma de Mallorca – as turbulent as it is historic – head southwest along the coast and pay a visit to the picturesque fishing villages of Sant Elm and Port d'Andratx. From here, we turn inland then over the Tramuntana Mountains to the west coast. We follow the coastline to Banyalbufar and explore the mountain range on an inward loop that takes us back to Andratx and ends at Banyalbufar again. We then enjoy a relaxing end to day one on the remaining kilometres to Valldemossa.

160 KM • 5 STUNDEN // 99 MILES • 5 HOURS

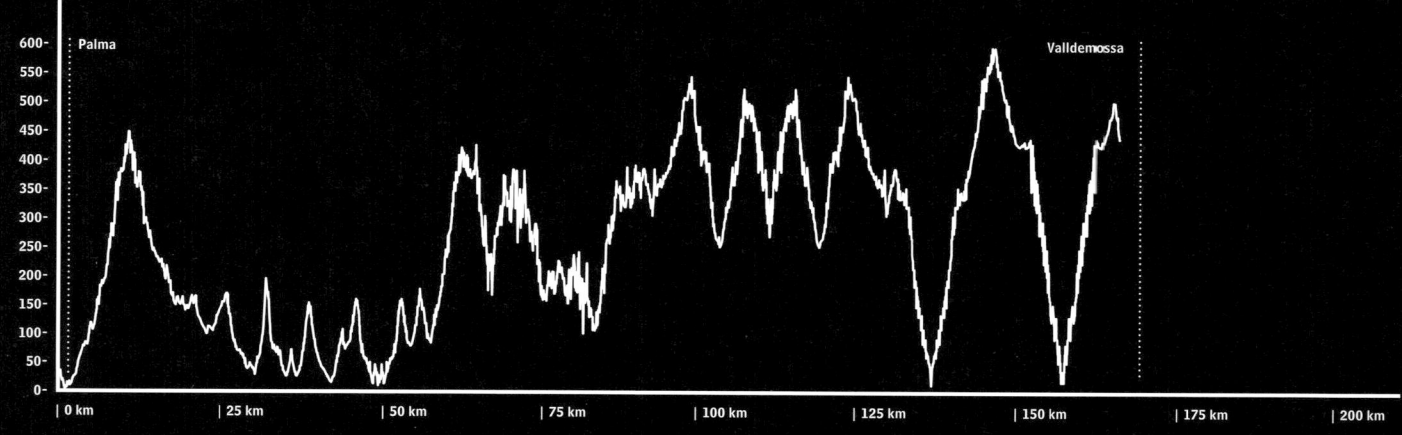

VALLDEMOSSA
LLUC

190 KM • 3,5 STUNDEN // 118 MILES • 3,5 HOURS

Guten Morgen, Valldemossa, Stadt hinter den Bergen. Wie ein Heiligenschein setzt die Morgensonne den Umrissen der Gebirgszüge im Westen Strahlenkränze auf. Das Meer leuchtet unwirklich blau. Vögel jagen zirpend, keckernd, zwitschernd um die Häuser. Durch Hinterhöfe mit Palmen und schattige Treppen.
—

Good morning, Valldemossa, the city on the other side of the mountains. The rays of morning sun frame the outline of the mountain range to the west like a halo. The sea glows a surreal blue. Birds dart chirping, chattering, twittering among the buildings. Through courtyards dotted with palm trees and shady steps.

HOTEL & RESTAURANT

HOTEL CA'N REUS
CARRER DE L'ALBA, 26
07109 FORNALUTX
TEL: +34 971 63 98 66
WWW.CANREUSHOTEL.COM

ESPLÉNDIDO HOTEL
ES TRAVES 5
07108 PUERTO DE SÓLLER
TEL: +34 971 63 18 50
FAX: +34 971 63 30 19
WWW.ESPLENDIDOHOTEL.COM

BIKINI ISLAND & MOUNTAIN HOTELS
CARRER DE MIGJORN, 2
TEL: +34 971 631700
WWW.BIKINI-HOTELS.COM

RESTAURANT NAMA
CARRER ARXIDUC LUÍS SALVADOR, 22,
07179 DEIÀ
WWW.RESTAURANTNAMA.COM
TEL: +34 971 63 61 02

Von der Straße ist das ruhige Plaudern der älteren Nachbarn zu hören, die sich dort auf ein Schwätzchen treffen, ganz zufällig natürlich, wie schon seit Jahren jeden Tag. Im Café gegenüber werden Stühle auf die Straße gerückt, ein Ober trägt ächzend die brusthohe Speisekarte ins Freie. „Obert", steht da mit weißer Kreide gemalt, „geöffnet".

Die ganze Szene schreit nach Frühstück, nach einem heißen Kaffee, nach frisch gepresstem Orangensaft und natürlich einem herzhaften Biss in die Ensaimada. Der Bäcker um die Ecke macht die mit Engelshaar, einer Kürbiskonfitüren-Füllung, die wohl deshalb so heißt, weil man bereits bei ihrem Anblick die Himmelsglocken läuten hört. Man könnte hierauf auch ein Cremadillo folgen lassen, bei dem sich jede Übersetzung oder Erklärung vermutlich erübrigt, und das wäre dann nur die Ouvertüre für den herzhaften Teil: geriebene Tomaten mit beinahe scharf schmeckendem Olivenöl auf dunklem Brot – wer jetzt noch nicht ins Genuss-Koma gefallen ist, könnte eine Käse-Sobrasada hinterherschieben, aber das müsste eigentlich schon nicht mehr sein. Könnte aber. Nur, um das gesagt zu haben. Theoretisch natürlich. Käse-Sobrasada.

From the street comes the quiet mumble of conversation among the elderly neighbours, who meet there for a chat – quite by accident, of course, as they have done every day for years. In the café opposite, chairs are being placed out on the pavement, a waiter groaning as he heaves a chest-high menu board outside, "Obert" emblazoned across it in white chalk – "open".

The entire scene screams breakfast – hot coffee, freshly squeezed orange juice and, of course, a hearty mouthful of Ensaimada. The bakery around the corner makes them with angel hair, a filling of pumpkin preserve that is apparently so called because just looking at it is enough to make you hear heavenly voices. You could follow that with a cremadillo, a translation or explanation of which is presumably unnecessary, which would be merely the overture for the main event – pureed tomatoes with olive oil that is almost spicy to the taste spread generously on a big slab of rustic, wholemeal bread. If this isn't enough to send you into a coma of sheer bliss, then how about adding a helping of cheese and sobrassada for good measure – no more surely? Well, maybe. Just to have said it. Purely theoretically.

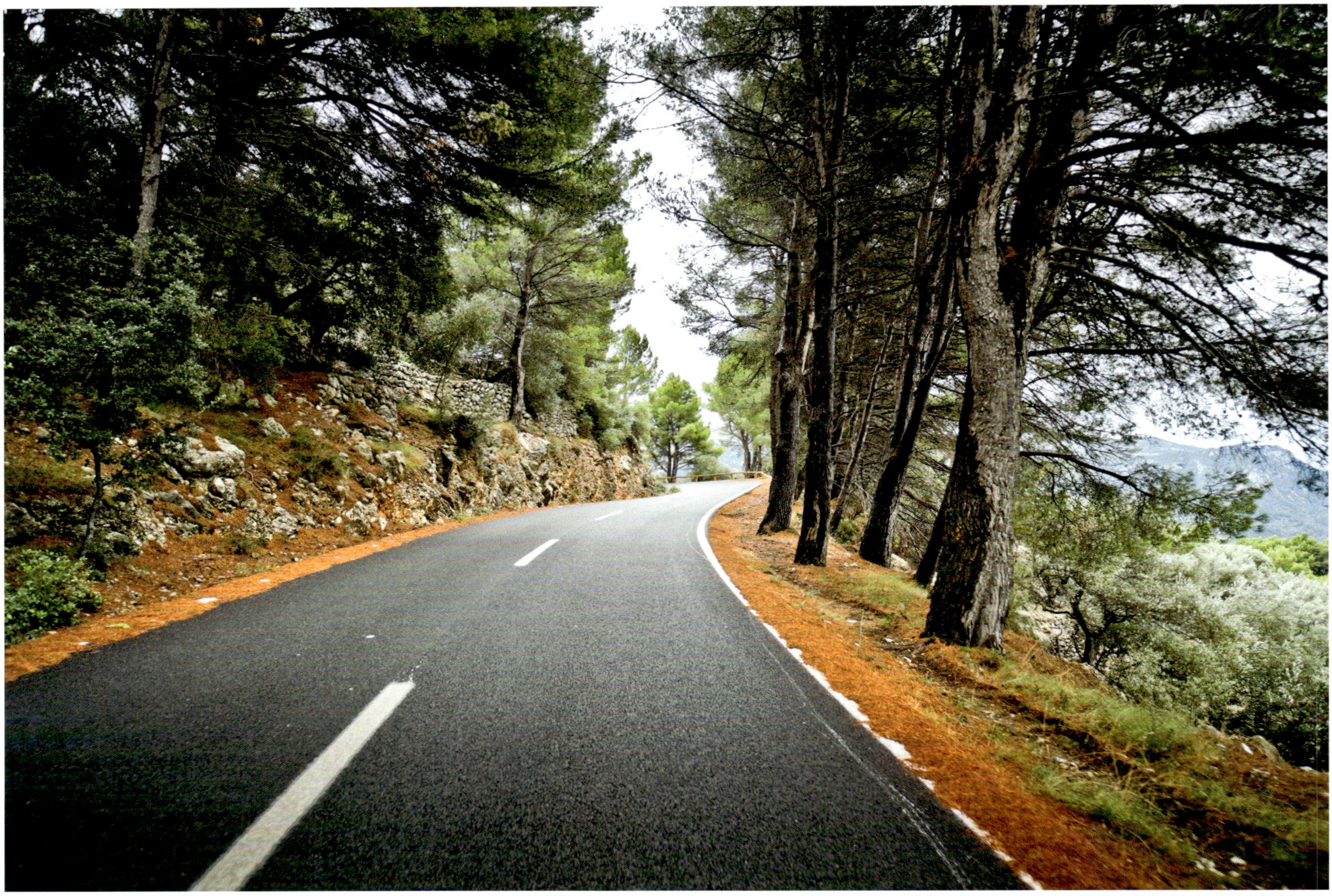

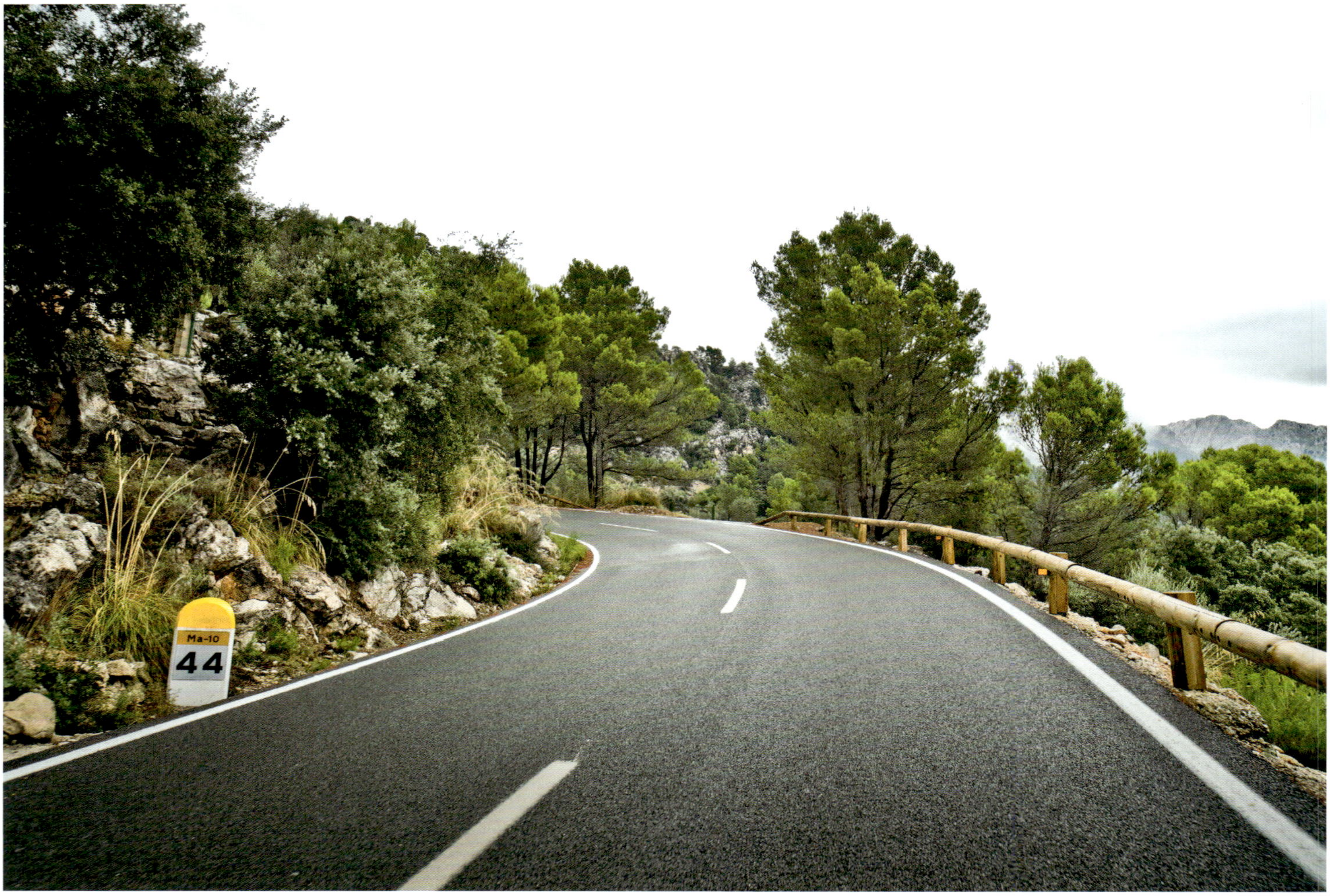
Ma-10
44

Klingt irgendwie schon gut, selbst wenn man gerade mit dem Tomatenbrot beschäftigt ist: süß und scharf und würzig. Also gut.

Es ist ja auch so: Für den zweiten Tag der Mallorca-Runde braucht man wieder ganz viel Kraft. Bereits die Überlegung, wie denn nun der mittlere Teil der Serra de Tramuntana zu absolvieren ist, das Filetstück sozusagen, verschlingt die Energie eines Helden. Im Uhrzeiger-Sinn oder dagegen? Gleich zum Serpentinenmonster nach Sa Calobra oder erst später? Am Nachmittag. – Genau dann fällt dem, der bereits die Sobrasada intus hat, ein, dass es ja wieder eine Runde ist. Und man deshalb einfach alles zweimal fahren kann. So ist Mallorca. Zuerst Frühstücken, dann Straßen-Achterbahn. Ein Paradies.

Zuerst aber rollen wir uns auf der Terrassenstraße über dem Meer ein. Ganz ruhig von Valldemossa nach Deià, das bildschön in den Hügeln liegt und froh sein kann, dass es der Sobrasada in unserem Magen genauso geht. Denn sonst wäre spätestens jetzt ein Überfall auf eine der kleinen Bäckereien angesagt, aus denen es nach frischem Brot duftet. So aber: weiter. Wieder Meer, wieder Steilabhang. Wegen einigen Verkehrs wieder nur ganz ruhiges Cruisen. Seitenscheibe runter. Ellbogen raus. Das gibt Punktabzug in der Haltungsnote, aber egal. Ist einfach richtig so. Morgens um halb zehn auf der Ma-10 hinter Deià, wenn die Sonne scheint. Und dann sind wir ja auch trotz des Bummeltempos schon bei Sóller angelangt, finden das von oben ganz wunderbar und rollen deshalb in Genießerlaune runter zum Hafen. Ein schneller Cafè geht ganz bestimmt. Muss gehen, denn ab jetzt sind Reflexe gefragt, wir stürmen hoch in Richtung Fornalutx. Das Meer bleibt hinter uns, wir schnüren ins Landesinnere, surfen die Kehren im Pinienwald und segeln durch Olivenhaine. Oleander und Kakteen sagen Benvinguts in Fornalutx, aber wir lassen das Dörfchen am Fuß des 1443 Meter hohen Puig Major rechts liegen, schneiden weiter auf der Ideallinie nach Osten. Es geht immer höher, immer weiter, das hört überhaupt nicht mehr auf. Wenn man in jeder Kurve die Luft anhalten müsste, wären wir längst erstickt, man würde uns finden, mit glücklichem Lächeln, die Hände ans Lenkrad

Cheese and sobrassada. Sounds pretty good actually, even when you're already busy with a chunk of bread and tomato. Sweet and hot and spicy – oh, alright then.

And let's face it – we need plenty of energy for the second day of our Majorca tour. Just the thought of covering that centre section of the Serra de Tramuntana – the fillet, you might say – is enough to sap the strength of heroes. Do we tackle it clockwise or anticlockwise? Do we head straight for the monster serpentine outside Sa Calobra or leave it until later – the afternoon, perhaps? It's at this point that it occurs to those who have already downed the sobrassada that it's yet another loop, meaning you can simply do it all twice. That's Majorca for you. First breakfast, then road rollercoaster. Sheer paradise.

But first, we take a gentle cruise along the terraced road above the sea. We take our time as we roll from Valldemossa to Deià, which nestles picturesquely in the hills and can rest assured that the sobrassada in our bellies is doing likewise. Because otherwise, now would be the ideal time for another onslaught on one of the small bakeries, enticing us with the smell of freshly baked bread. But no – we press onwards. More sea, more steep mountainsides. A bit of traffic means we're cruising gently again – windows rolled down, elbows out. Points are deducted from our performance score for that, but who cares. It's simply the right thing to do. It's half past nine in the morning on the Ma-10 outside Deià and the sun is shining. And despite the easy-going tempo, we're in Sóller in no time. It looks fabulous from above and, with a song in our hearts, we decide to cruise down to the harbour.

There's surely time for a quick coffee. There has to be – from here on in it's all about reflexes as we dash upwards heading for Fornalutx. We leave the sea behind us as we wind inland, surfing the hairpins in the pine forest and gliding through olive groves. Oleander and cacti say "benvinguts" to Fornalutx, but we pass on by the village at the foot of the 1443-metre Puig Major, staying on the ideal line eastwards. The road takes us higher and higher, farther

SA CALOBRA

BAR „COLL DELS REIS"

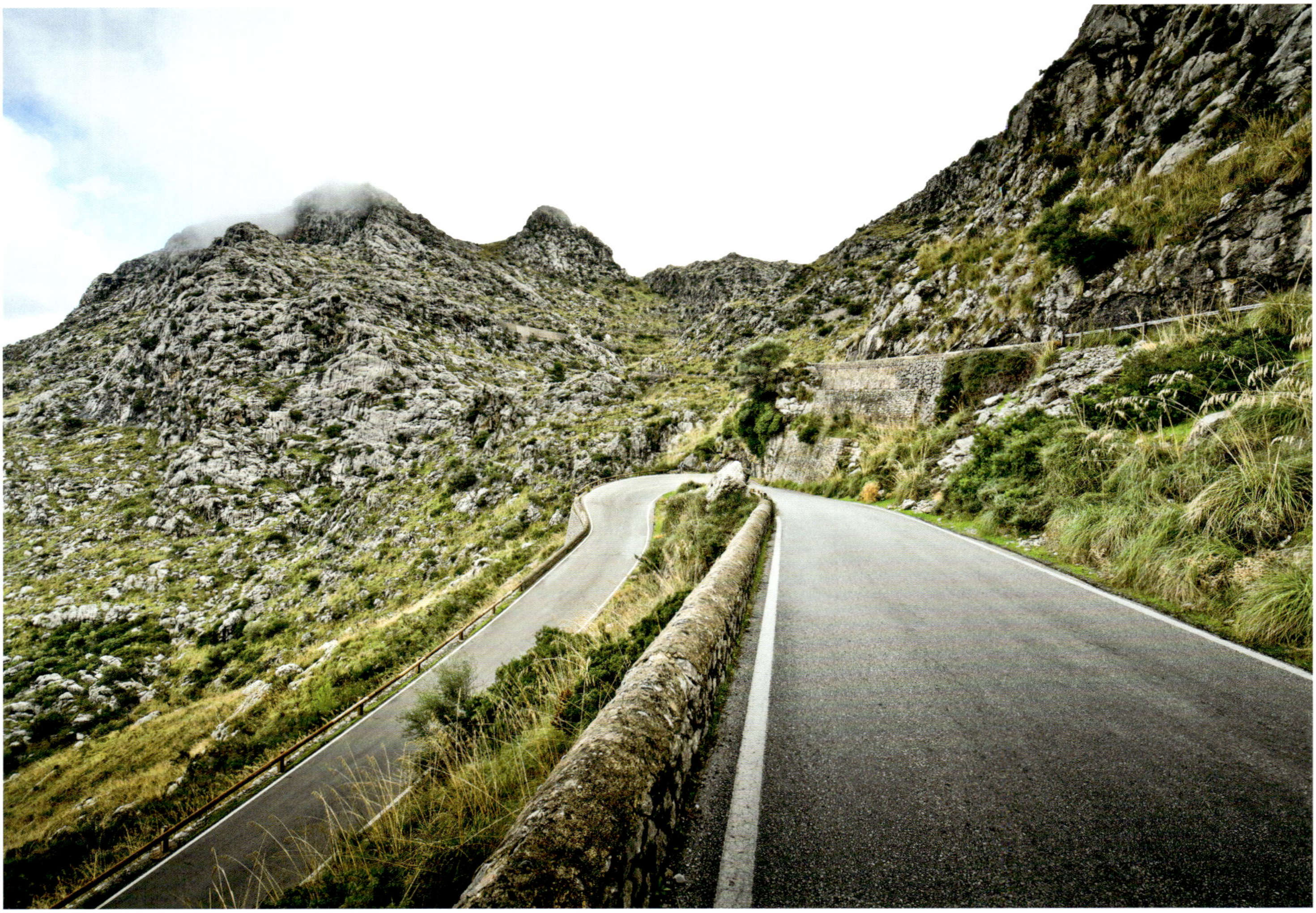

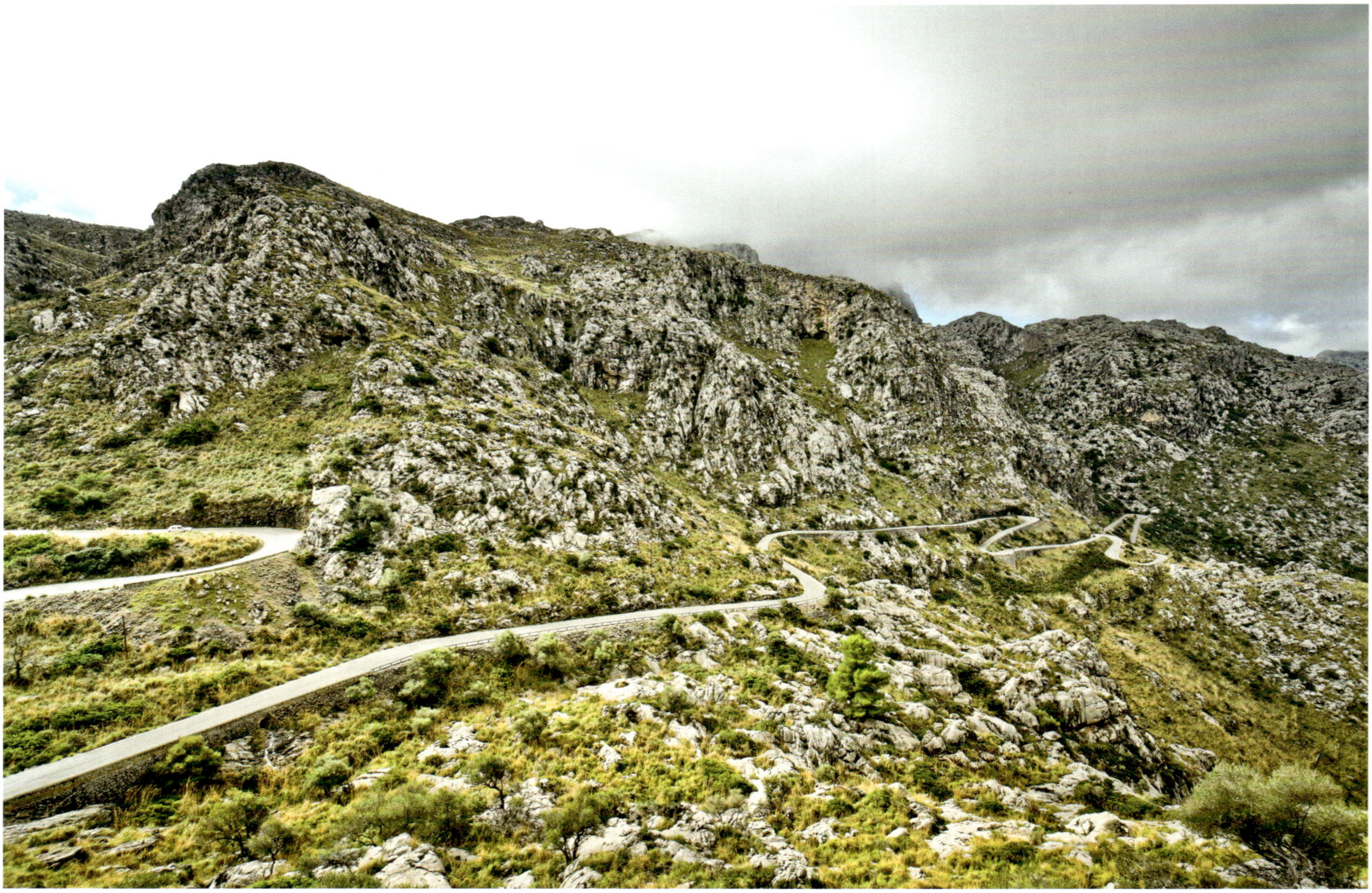

geklammert und mit laufendem Motor. Der Beifahrer spricht aus, was alle denken. Sein Kommentar zu diesem atemlosen Kurvengetümmel auf Premium-Asphalt ist ungemein treffend: Mannomann, sagt er, und dann nochmal: Mannomann. Ungläubiges Kopfschütteln, fassungsloses Lächeln. Aber dann ist die Straße auch schon unter der Felswand an den südlichen Zinnen des Puig-Major-Massivs und hechtet in den Tunnel de Monnaber. Man muss hier aufpassen: Es ist zu Beginn zappenduster, also Licht immer anlassen, denn bestimmt strampeln dann genau in dem Moment fröhlich pfeifend ein paar Rennradler durch die Röhre, die sich über die flachen Meter im kühlen Tunnel freuen, aber natürlich kein Licht am Rad haben. Morgens um 11 auf Mallorca. Warum auch?

Rüber zum Stausee Gorg Blau und jetzt hat sich die ganze Landschaft geändert. Wir sind im gleißenden Inneren einer kalkweißen Gebirgswelt angelangt, in der Vegetation gerade geduldet wird. Gräser in trockenen, windzerzausten Büscheln. Gestrüpp. Hartes Strauchwerk. Knorrige Bäume. Schnell wieder durch den nächsten Tunnel nach Westen in ein Zwischental und vor dem alten Viadukt links abbiegen. Sa Calobra. Entschlossen steigt die schmale Straße den Berg hinauf, kurvt und schraubt sich quer der kargen Hänge immer weiter in die Höhe. Richtig steil wird es hier nie, aber das schmale, hartnäckige Asphaltband hat trotzdem eine bedrohliche Ausstrahlung, die durch die felsige Landschaft ringsum regelrecht verstärkt wird. Und dann sind da ja noch die Kurven. Die Straßenbauer scheinen nach Kurven, Kehren und Serpentinennadeln bezahlt worden zu sein, jede Verwerfung im Gelände wird abgesurft, jede Höhenlinie darf zur Geltung kommen. Den Vogel schießt die überbrückte/untertunnelte Schleifchen-Kehre nach dem Coll dels Reis ab, die es prominent sogar ins Programm der durchgeknallten britischen TV-Show „Grand Tour" geschafft hat. Rennen Auto gegen Skateboard. Ja, genau, das war hier. Leider können wir die Strasse nicht sperren. Gerade jetzt schält sich da vorne ein Reisebus vom Parkplatz, um unerschütterlich im Zeitlupentempo weiter den Berg nach Port de Sa Calobra hinunterzustampfen. Jetzt bloß nicht die Nerven verlieren und

and farther – it never seems to end. If you had to hold your breath around every bend, we would have long suffocated. They would find us with happy smiles on our faces, hands clutching the steering wheel and the engine running. The man in the passenger seat says what everybody else is thinking. His comment on this breathless turmoil of twists and turns on premium asphalt is totally on point: "Wow," he says, followed by "Wow." A disbelieving shake of the head, a stunned grin. But then the road sweeps beneath the southern rockface of the Puig Major and into the Tunnel de Monnaber. You have to be really on your game here. It starts off pitch black so turn the lights on. Here is precisely when a couple of racing cyclists are most likely to pedal into the pipe whistling merrily; pleased to be riding on the flat for a while through the coolness of the tunnel, but obviously with no lights on their bikes. It's 11 o'clock in the morning on Majorca. Why would they?

We head over to the Gorg Blau reservoir, where the scenery is totally different. We've landed in the glistening interior of a chalk-white mountain landscape, where vegetation is more-or-less tolerated. Tufts of dry, windswept grass. Scrubland. Ragged shrubs. Gnarled trees. We're soon in the next tunnel heading westward into another valley then turn left just before the old viaduct. Sa Calobra. The narrow road clambers resolutely up the mountainside, twisting and turning its way upwards along the sparse slopes. At no point is it ever really steep, but the narrow, persistent strip of asphalt nevertheless has a threatening demeanour, distinctly amplified by the rocky landscape round about. And then there's the curves. It seems like the road builders are paid per bend, hairpin and serpentine needle. Every drop in the terrain is surfed, every contour emphasised. What beggars belief, however, is the bridged and tunnelled series of bends at the Coll dels Reis, which even featured in off-the-wall British TV show "Grand Tour". Race car versus skateboard. Yup, that was here.

Unfortunately, we can't close off the mountain. Right in front of us, a coach swings out of a car park to continue undeterred its slow-mo stomp down the mountainside to

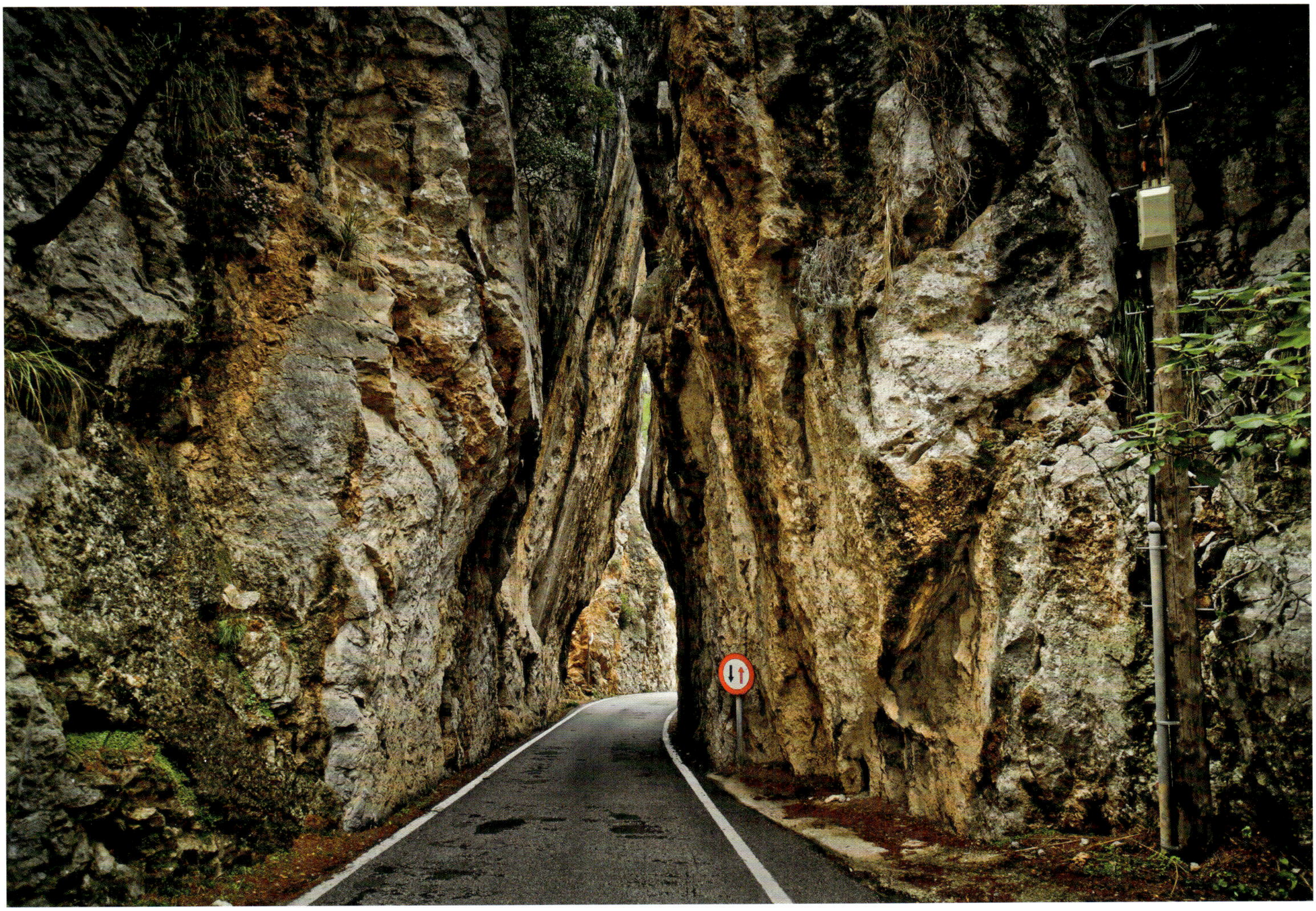

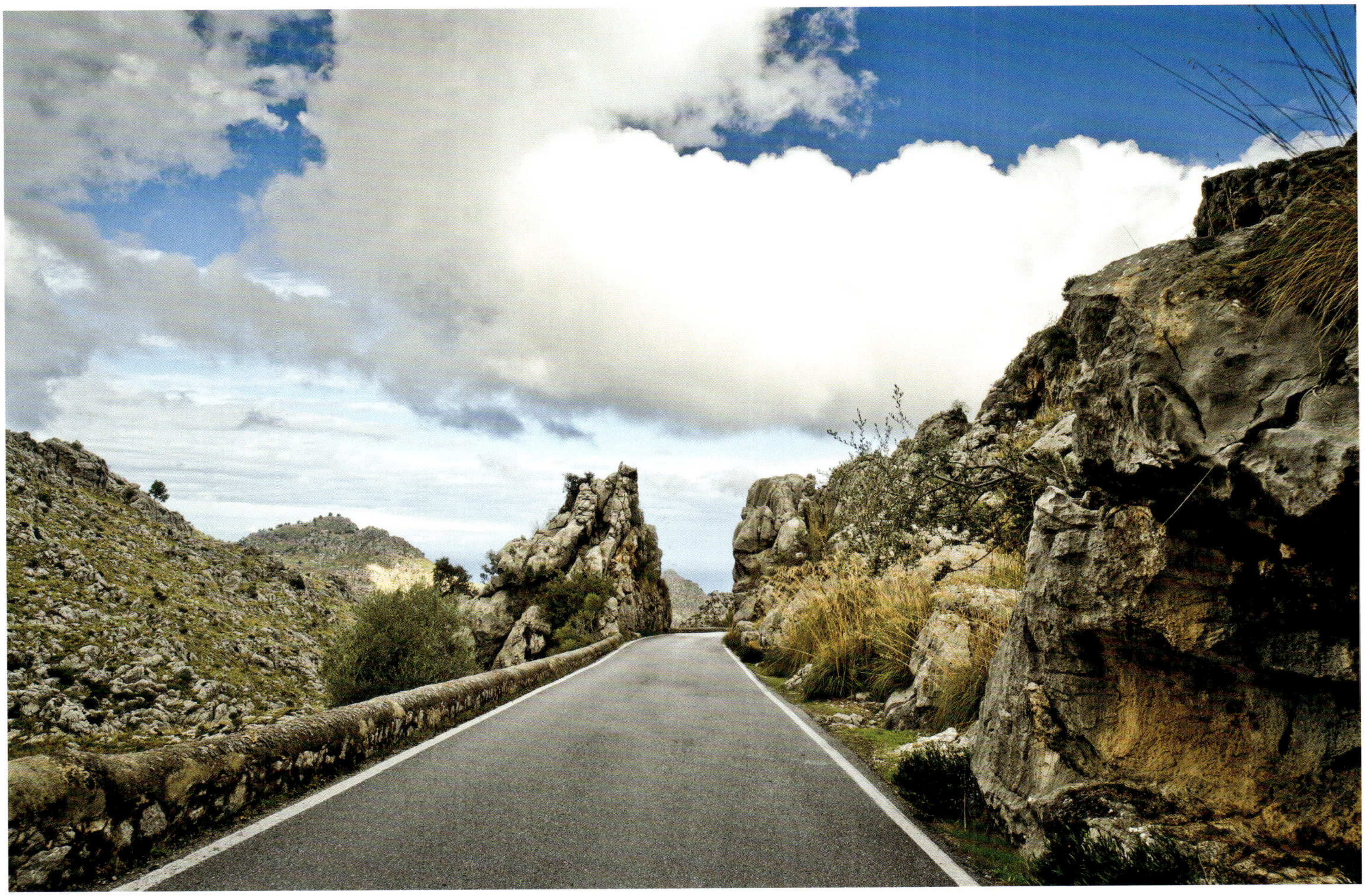

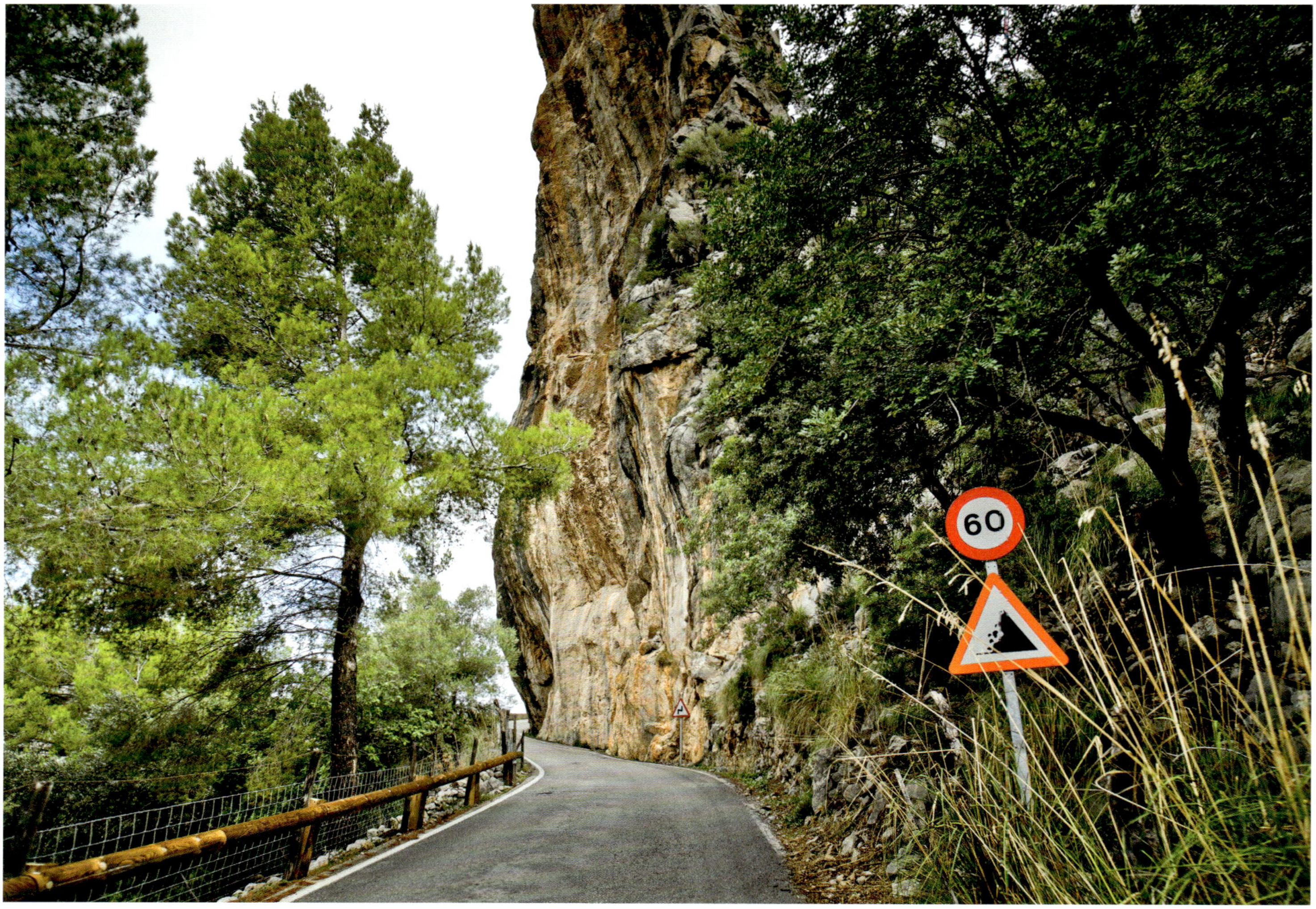
60

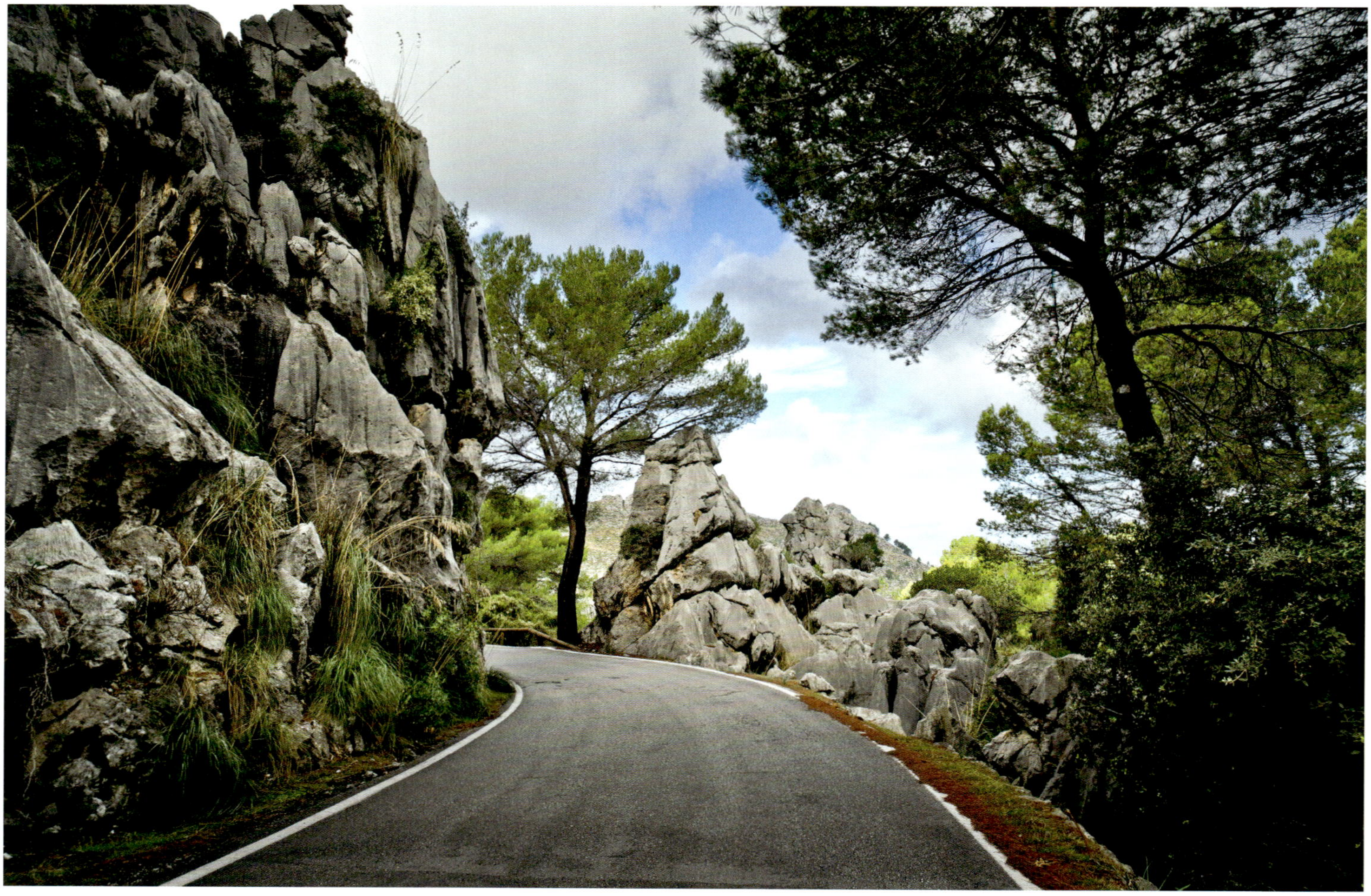

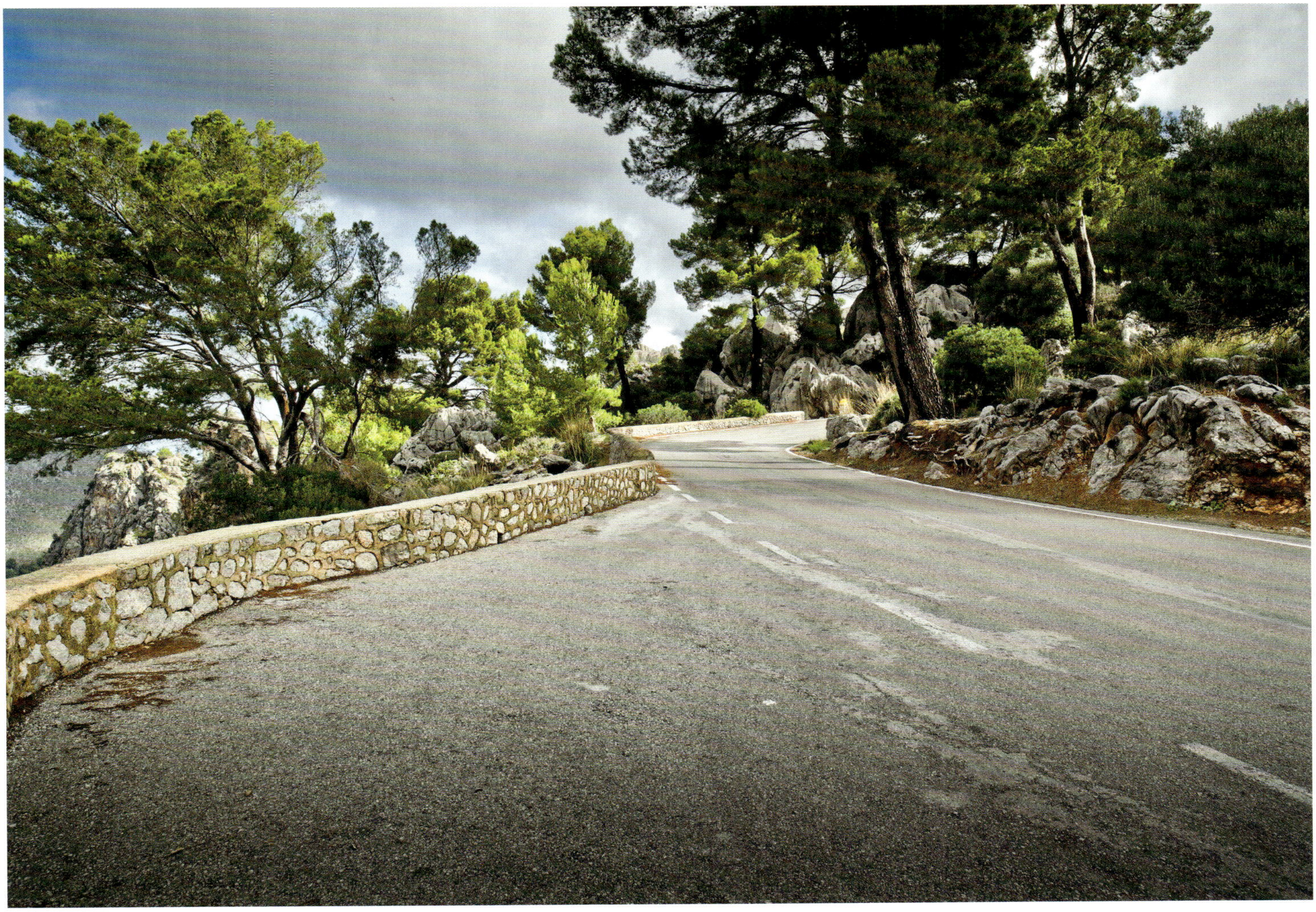

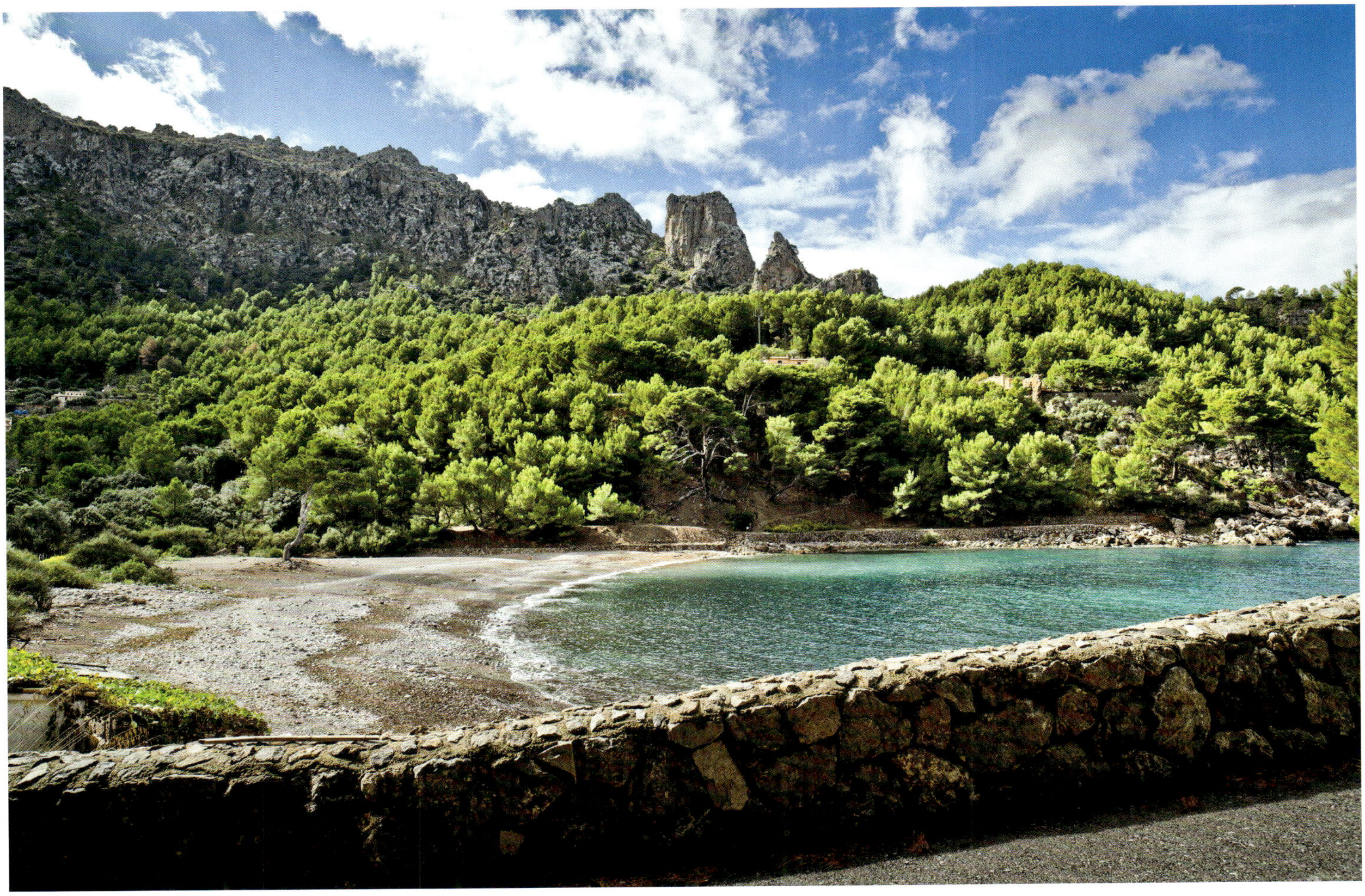

Die Straßenbauer scheinen nach Kurven, Kehren und Serpentinennadeln bezahlt worden zu sein, jede Verwerfung im Gelände wird abgesurft, jede Höhenlinie darf zur Geltung kommen. Den Vogel schießt die überbrückte/untertunnelte Schleifchen-Kehre nach dem Coll dels Reis ab, die es prominent sogar ins Programm der durchgeknallten britischen TV-Show „Grand Tour" geschafft hat.

It seems like the road builders are paid per bend, hairpin and serpentine needle. Every drop in the terrain is surfed, every contour emphasised. What beggars belief, however, is the bridged and tunnelled series of bends at the Coll dels Reis, which even featured in off-the-wall British TV show "Grand Tour".

womöglich hupend hinterherschleichen. Stattdessen: Pause machen. Die milde Bergluft genießen. Tief durchatmen. Und dann einen infamen Plan aushecken. Zum Beispiel so: In ungefähr 25 Minuten dürfte der Bus unten am Hafen sein. Es folgt eine halbe Stunde, in der Busreisende Andenken-Nippes kaufen. Dann dauert es noch einmal fünf Minuten bis auch der Letzte vom Klo zurück ist und den Bus gefunden hat. Bis spätestens dann müsste man unten gewesen sein, um eine Gruppe Genussradler zu überreden, genau jetzt den Berg in Angriff zu nehmen. Auf ganzer Streckenbreite. Schön gemütlich. Direkt vor dem Bus. Eine Stunde lang ohne Verkehr von hinten radeln, herrlich entspannt. Die müssten einfach nur das Schluchzen der Businsassen hinter sich überhören und die Kaugeräusche des sein Lenkrad verzehrenden Busfahrers. So süß könnte Rache sein. Zuckersüß wie ein Cremadillo.

Wir warten eine Viertelstunde, rocken dann den Berg runter und lassen die netten Leute aus dem Bus unser cooles Auto bestaunen. Der Busfahrer schaut ziemlich unglücklich, als wir wieder losstarten. Beschleunigung, erster Gang, Vroam, zweiter Gang, Vroam, dritter Gang, Vroam. Pures Glück. Armer Kerl. Schwungvoll rollen wir über den Berg

Port de Sa Calobra. Don't lose your nerve now; don't take this personally and hang on his tail the whole way down honking the horn. Instead – take a break and enjoy the mild mountain air. Breathe deeply. And then come up with a cunning plan, Perhaps something like this: The coach will surely take around 25 minutes to reach the port. Then comes half an hour, during which its passengers will buy souvenir knick-knacks. Then it will take another five minutes for the stragglers to make it back from the toilets and onto the bus. We have to be down there by no later than that to convince a group of pleasure cyclists to tackle the mountain ... right now. To spread themselves across the full width of the road and take their time. Right in front of the bus. They can cycle for a whole hour without any traffic from behind, nice and easy.

They just shouldn't pay any heed to the sobbing of the bus passengers behind them and the crunching of the bus driver chewing on his steering wheel. Revenge can be so sweet. As sugar-sweet as a Cremadillo.

We wait quarter of an hour before tearing down the mountain and then letting the nice people from the bus admire our cool car. The bus driver looks pretty unhappy

COLL DE SÓLLER

COLL DE SÓLLER

zurück ins Landesinnere, biegen im Städtchen Selva mit seinen Tafones, alten Ölmühlen, nach links ab, um Inca zu umfahren. Hier werden später unsere Bus-Freunde die „cellars" stürmen, um deftige, ländliche Gerichte mit regionalem Wein hinunterzuspülen. Wir sind dann schon an Lloseta vorbei, haben vor Alaró die Straße zum Castell d'Alaró genommen und über den kleinen Weiler Orient die Berge zurückerobert. Man könnte jetzt in den arabischen Jardins d'Alfàbia eine Pause einlegen, aber wir haben ja noch ein Rendezvous. Mit dem bösen Bruder der Straße nach Sa Calobra, einem wahren Kurvenmonster, schieläugig, warzig und behaart. Es heißt Coll de Sóller, ist nach alpinen Maßstäben harmlose 497 Meter hoch, gefühlt aber ein Fahrspaß-Dreitausender. Der Pass zwischen der großen Zentralebene Pla de Mallorca und dem Sóller-Tal sammelt auf kaum sieben Kilometern eine Unzahl von Kurven und Kehren, zieht Rennradfahrer an wie ein Glas Honigbienen und muss jetzt einfach sein. Einmal, weil das eben der kürzeste Weg nach Sóller und in den Norden ist, andererseits aber auch, weil wir genau wegen Straßen wie dieser auf Mallorca sind. Vergnügungssteuerpflichtiger Spaß ab 18, eine echte Droge.

Drüben in Sóller angekommen ist der Tag dann rund, uns fällt nichts ein, was jetzt noch kommen könnte. Gelassen surfen wir die bekannte Route unterhalb des Puig Major, fühlen uns gereift und entspannt, Sturm und Drang sind vollkommen abgefallen. Wir schielen in die Restaurants, feuern Rennradfahrer an, genießen den Nachmittag. In Lluc ist Schluß. Mehr Mallorca verkraften wir heute nicht mehr. Außer vielleicht kulinarisch. Aber das ist eine andere Geschichte.

when we set off again. Acceleration, first gear, vrooooom, second gear, vrooooom, third gear, vrooooom. Sheer joy. Poor guy. We sweep back inland, up over the mountain, taking a left in the town of Selva with its "tafones" (old oil mills) to avoid Inca, where our bus friends will later storm the cellars to wash down hearty country food with region wine. We've already passed Lloseta, taking the road to Castell d' Alaró just before we reach Alaró to win back the mountains via the small hamlet of Orient. We could stop for a bit in the Arabian Jardins d'Alfàbia, but we have a rendezvous; with the evil brother of the road to Sa Calobra, a veritable curve monster – cross-eyed, warty and hairy. It's called Coll de Sóller. By Alpine standards, it's a harmless 497 metres high but feels like a high-revving three-thousander. The pass between the big central plain of Pla de Mallorca and the Sóller valley packs countless bends and hairpins into barely seven kilometres, draws racing cyclists like honeybees and is an absolute must. For one thing, because it's the shortest route to Sóller and the north of the island and, for another, because roads like this are precisely the reason we're here on Majorca in the first place. Fun for over-18s, subject to amusement tax – a real drug.

Once we reach Sóller, the day is done. We can't think of anything else we could possibly do now. We glide gently along the familiar route beneath the Puig Major, feeling fulfilled and relaxed. All sense of urgency and perseverance subside. We peer into restaurants, cheer on cyclists, enjoy the afternoon. We call it a day in Lluc. We won't manage any more of Majorca today – other than maybe on a culinary level. But that's another story.

RESTAURANT

CA NA TO NE TA
HORITZÓ 21
07314 CAIMARI
TELEFON: +34 971 515 226
WWW.CANATONETA.COM

HOTEL

FINCA ES CASTELL
CTRA. CAIMARI-MANCOR
07313 SELVA
TELEFON: +34 971 87 51 54
WWW.FINCAESCASTELL.COM

1902 TOWNHOUSE
07100 SÓLLER
TEL: +34 658 841 648
WWW.HOTEL1902SOLLER.COM

CA'N ISABEL
CALLE ISABEL II , 13
07100 SÓLLER
TEL: +34 971 638 097

VALLDEMOSSA LLUC

Auf der zweiten Etappe beschäftigen wir uns hauptsächlich mit dem zentralen Teil des Gebirges der Serra de Tramuntana. Vom Start in Valldemossa bewegen wir uns zuerst noch einige Kilometer mit großartiger Aussicht auf das Mittelmeer in Richtung Sóller, ab hier verläuft die Route aber hinein in die Berge. Über das Gebirgs-städtchen Fornalutx und eine zweimalige Tunnel-Unterquerung des Puig Major-Massivs gelangen wir wieder zurück ans Meer. Vorher darf aber die schmale Serpentinen-Strecke nach Sa Calobra genossen werden, die besonders außerhalb der Touristen-Hochsaison oder am frühen Morgen und späten Abend puren Fahrspaß und Kurven satt bietet. Von hier aus überqueren wir das Gebirge erneut, halten uns dann in den Hügeln am Fuß der Tramuntana zurück nach Südwesten, um nach der Überquerung des Coll de Sóller zusammen mit der alten Eisenbahn aus Palma de Mallorca die Runde nach Sóller abzuschließen. Ein abschließender Loop nach Nordosten schließt die Runde ab und bringt uns zum Ausgang der zweiten Etappe beim Kloster Lluc.

—

On the second section of our journey, we cover mainly the centre part of the Serra de Tramuntana mountain range. From our starting point in Valldemossa, we first spend a few kilometres heading for Sóller with an amazing view of the Mediterranean, after which the route leads into the mountains. We return to the sea via the mountain village of Fornalutx and two tunnels through the Puig Major mountain. But first, we were able to enjoy the delights of the narrow Sa Calobra serpentine, which offers sheer driving joy and curves galore, especially out of the main tourist season or in the early morning or late evening. From here, we cross back over the mountains then linger in the hills at the foot of the Tramuntana heading southwest again to complete the loop to Sóller, after crossing the Coll de Sóller, alongside the old railway line from Palma de Mallorca. We finish the tour by looping to the northeast and ending the second stage at the Lluc Monastery.

190 KM • 3,5 STUNDEN // 118 MILES • 3,5 HOURS

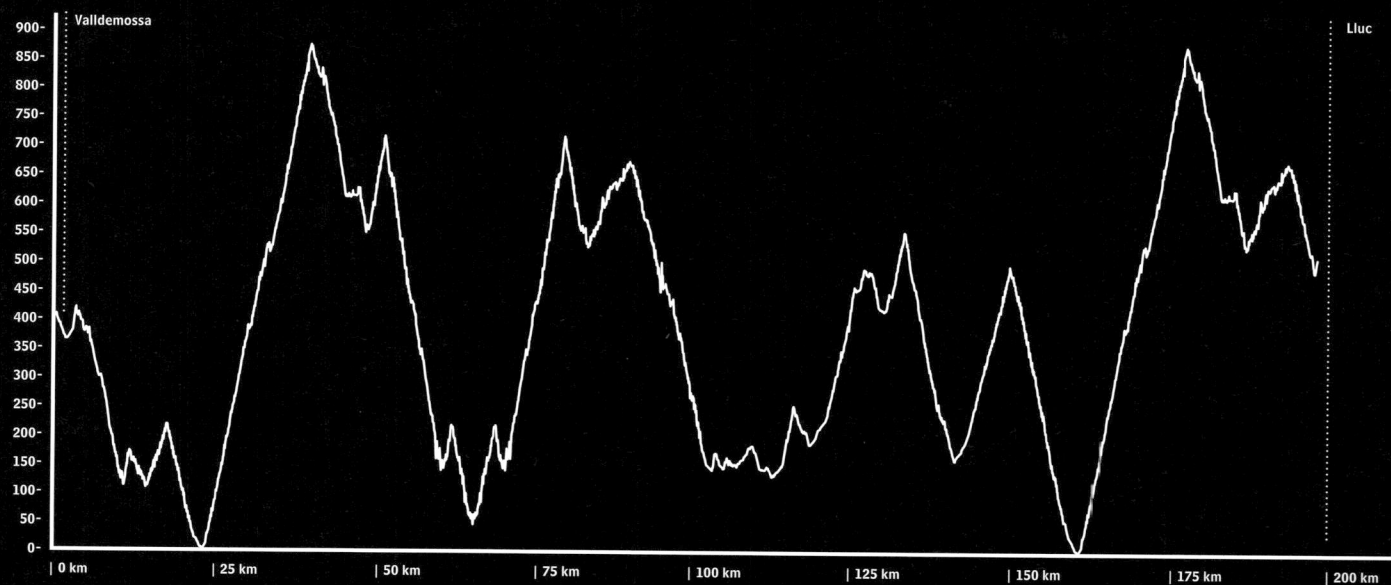

LLUC
PORTO CRISTO

193 KM • 5,5 STUNDEN // 119 MILES • 5,5 HOURS

500 Meter über dem Meer, in den Bergen der Serra de Tramuntana, ist Mallorca uralt und beladen mit Geschichten. Das Santuari de Santa Maria de Lluc möchte beinahe 800 Jahre alt sein, die kleine, dunkle Marienstatue in ihrem Inneren umweht eine kaum zu glaubende Legende.
—

500 meters above the sea, in the mountains of the Serra de Tramuntana, Majorca is ancient and steeped in history. The Santuari de Santa Maria de Lluc is close to 800 years old. The small, dark statue of Mary inside is cloaked in an almost unbelievable legend

Deshalb darf jetzt auch die kurze Wallfahrt vom Parkplatz des Heiligtums hinein in die Basilika nicht fehlen, quer durch den Kirchenraum und dann in die hintere Seitenkapelle. Dort steht die dunkle Madonna und scheint etwas zu wissen, das die Betrachter nicht wissen. Sie lächelt seit 1229, was hat sie nicht alles gesehen? Und lächelt immer noch. So schlimm kann es also nicht sein mit der Welt.

Kalter Stein, eine Ahnung der Körpergeruchs-Melange von Besuchern aus Jahrzehnten, mürbes Kerzenwachs-Aroma. Es ist ein weiter Weg aus dem frühen Mittelalter in die Postmoderne. Es ist auch ein weiter Weg aus der Ewigkeit zurück in den Augenblick. Jeder Schritt bedeutet Vergessen. Auftauchen. Oder doch Abtauchen? Was ist real? Transzendenz oder Immanenz? Es ist ein Gedanke, der einem selten über den Weg läuft und nicht einmal ins Innere einer Kirche gehört. Wenn er einen aber streift, bleibt eine kleine Wehmut zurück. Als könne man für einen kurzen Moment etwas erfassen. Die Zusammenhänge, das Wesen aller Dinge, die Pointe des Seins. Im nächsten Moment ist aber alles verflogen, wie ein absurder Traum im Moment des Aufwachens. Wenn man dann durch die alten Holztüren am Portal zurück ins Freie stolpert, fällt die kühle Luft der Basilika ab wie ein Schleier. Der frische Duft des Tals und warme Sonnenstrahlen werden zur Erinnerung an die Gegenwart. Über das grobe Pflaster des Hofs gehen wir zuerst unsicher, dann lächelnd. „It's only Rock 'n' Roll but I like it, like it, yes I do", summt jemand und lacht plötzlich. Passt überhaupt nicht hierher. Oder vielleicht gerade doch.

So oder so geht es jetzt durch die Berge, schwingend und surfend der Ma-10 nach, die Tramuntana zeigt sich noch einmal von ihrer besten Seite. Sanfte Kurvenschwünge mit sattem Groove ziehen sich runter bis nach Pollença, am Fuß des Gebirges. Ein Pulk Rennradfahrer huldigt vor uns dem Gott des Speed, segelt Lenker an Lenker durch die Kehren, vollzieht ein spannendes Positionswechsel-Ballett mit zartem Hanging-Off, powert sich dann beim brachialen Pedalieren auf den Geraden vollkommen aus. Man nennt das wohl

Let´s do a short pilgrimage from the sanctuary's car park into the basilica, right through the interior of the church and into the side chapel at the back. There stands the dark Madonna, appearing to know something that the beholder does not. She has been smiling since 1229. The things she must have seen in that time – and yet she's still smiling. The world can't be that bad after all.

Cold stone, a hint of the scent-melange of decades of visitors and musty candlewax. It's a long way from the Middle Ages to the Post-Modern. It's also a long way from eternity back to the moment. Every step means forgetting. Emerging. Or maybe descending? What is real? Transcendence or imminence? It's a thought that rarely crosses one's path and that certainly doesn't belong inside a church. But when it touches you, it leaves behind a slight pang of melancholy – as if, just for a brief moment, you could capture something. The correlations, the essence of all things, the point of existence. But it all evaporates in an instant, like an absurd dream in that moment of waking. When you then stumble back into the open through the old wooden doors of the portal, the cool air of the basilica falls away like a veil. The fresh scent of the valley and warm rays of sun become a reminder of the present. We walk across the rough cobbles of the courtyard initially with a degree of uncertainty and then smiling. Someone is humming: "It's only rock 'n' roll but I like it, like it, yes I do," followed by a sudden laugh. Totally unbecoming to this situation – or then again, maybe not.

Either way, it's time now to head for the hills, sweeping and surfing along the Ma-10, the Tramuntana once again showing their best side. Gentle, sweeping curves with a satisfying groove lead down to Pollenca at the foot of the mountains. A huddle of cyclists in front of us are worshipping the god of speed, gliding handlebar-to-handle-bar through bends, executing a thrilling positional ballet with a delicate peeling-off manoeuvre, before powering along the straights with a burst of furious pedalling. You could call it an illegal road race, but it is a pleasure to watch this impressive co-operative from behind. At least, until we're

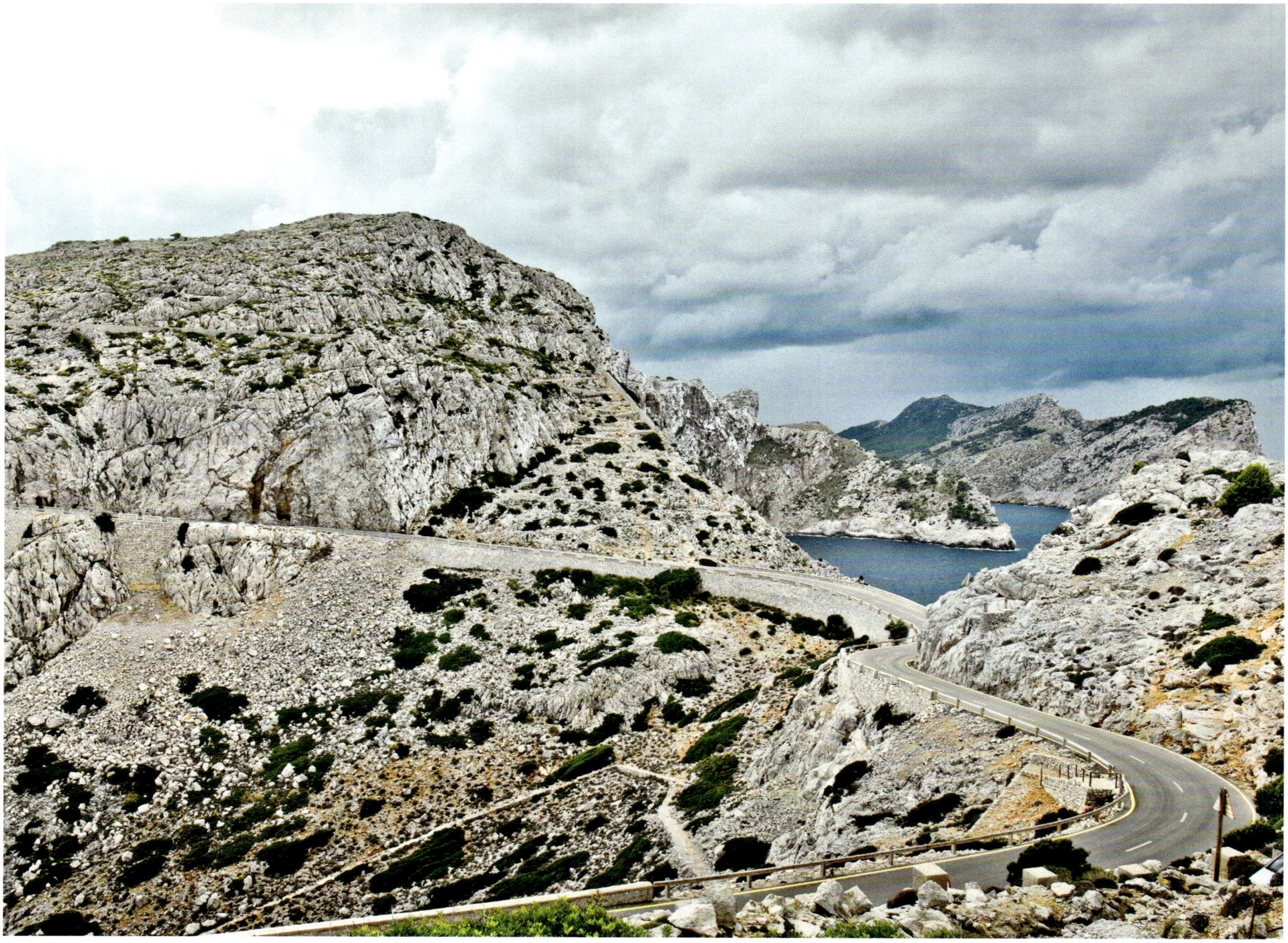

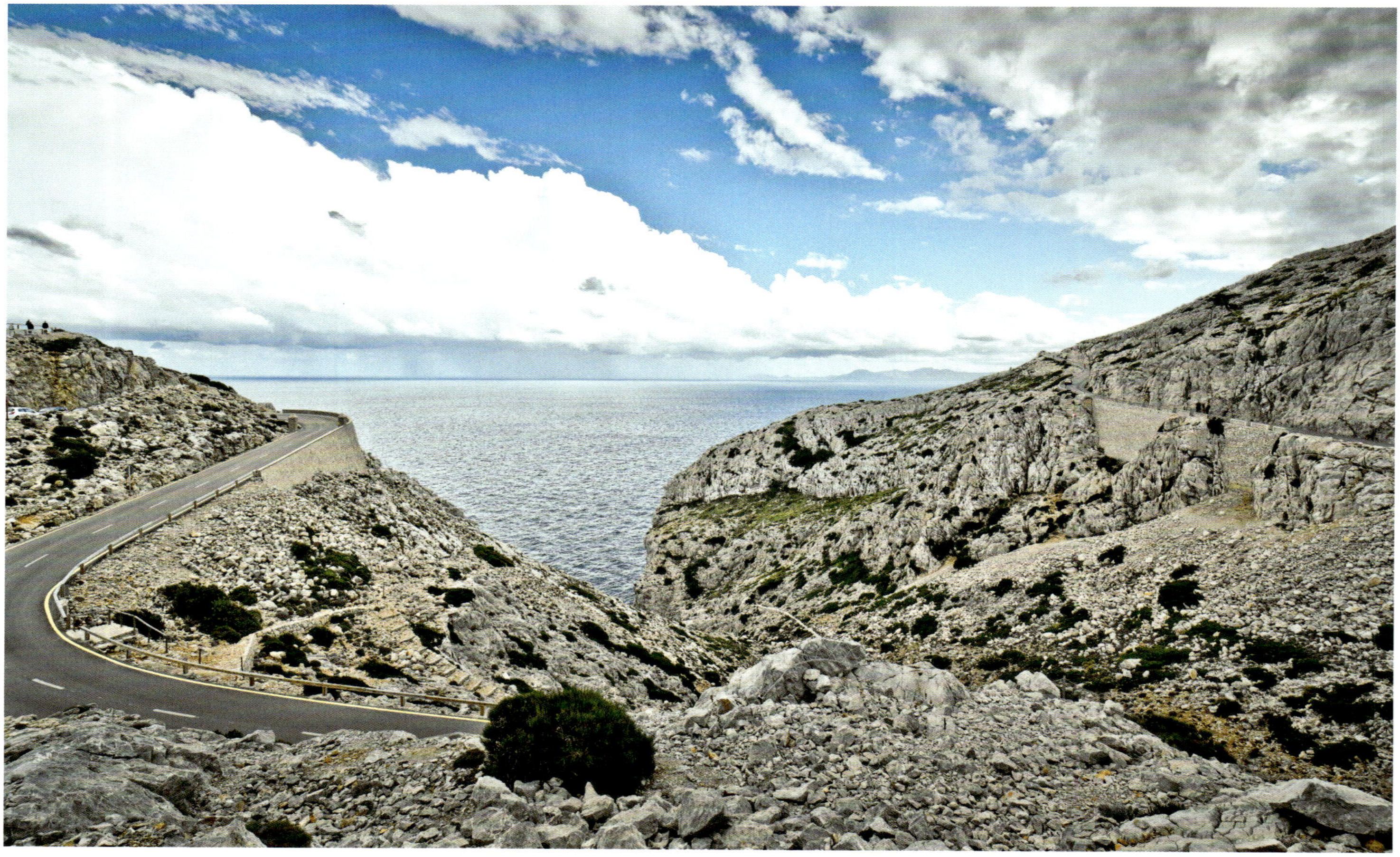

ein illegales Straßenrennen, aber es macht Freude, sich diese heiße Kiste von hinten anzusehen. Zumindest so lange, bis wir unten im Tal sind und die Meute im Bannstrahl der Ebene plötzlich wieder friedlich wird. Überholen, Gruß aus dem Seitenfenster an die seelenverwandten Kurven-Freunde.

Wir lassen die Stadt rechts liegen. Trudeln nach der Einsamkeit der vorherigen Berg-Etappen etwas verstört durch den Einkaufszentren-Tankstellen-Gürtel am Ortsrand und streben dann auch am Hafen von Pollença vorbei. Wir umrunden entschlossen die Bucht und stechen dann direkt am Ortsende von Port de Pollença geradeaus zurück in die Berge. Der letzte Ausläufer des Gebirges hat jetzt noch knapp 20 Kilometer Zeit, um sich richtig auszutoben, auf dem nördlichsten Zipfel der gesamten Insel geht es noch einmal höchst dramatisch bis zum Cap de Formentor. Hinter uns bleibt der Hafen von Pollença zurück, hinein ins Tal zum Wachtturm von Es Colomer. Die Straße pfeilt am Berghang entlang, ringsherum klettert Dickicht über groben Fels. Nach ein paar Wechselschwüngen unterhalb des Turms sind wir auch schon wieder direkt zurück am Meer, das azurblau und babybadewannenwasserwarm in der Bucht des Platja de Formentor schwappt.

Eine lange Allee von Pinien, Eichen, Oliven saugt uns dann weiter auf die Halbinsel hinaus, die schmale und schnurgerade Straße ist allerdings nach wenigen Kilometern zurück unter riesigen Felsformationen, die nun zu umrunden sind. Ein, zwei Serpentinenschwünge in die Höhe, ran an den Fels, tief unten tun sich die einsamen Buchten an der Küste des Kaps auf. Dann schneidet die Straße in den Stein, huscht unterhalb des Massivs aufs nächste Aussichtsniveau und löst schlagartig ein Déjà-vu aus: So sieht es immer wieder auch an der berühmten US-Küstenstraße aus. Highway Number One, Pacific Coast Highway im Taschenformat auf Mallorca. Was es nicht alles gibt.

Weiter, immer weiter. Das äußerste Ende im Norden Mallorcas ist schroff und stolz, gemacht aus kargem Fels, auf den eine schmale Straße führt, mit Kurven und Kehren

down in the valley and the pack suddenly settles back down in the anathema of a flat road. We overtake, waving casually to our curve-riding soulmates from the side window.

We pass on through the town. Following the solitude of the mountain stages we've just done, we amble somewhat perturbed through the shopping malls and fuel stations surrounding the town and continue on past Pollenca harbour, too. With our minds set, we circle the bay and then, as soon as we leave Port de Pollenca, head straight back into the mountains. The final foothills of the mountains still offer almost 20 more kilometres for us to get stuck into. At the island's northernmost tip is another incredibly dramatic section taking us to Cap de Formentor. Pollenca harbour is behind us as we head into the valley towards the Es Colomer watchtower. The road clings to the side of the mountain, surrounded by a tangle of brush clambering over the rugged rockface. After a couple of alternating bends beneath the tower, we're right back at the sea again – azure blue, warm as a baby's bathwater and lapping gently along the bay of Platja de Formentor.

A long avenue of pine, oak and olive trees draws us further along the peninsula. However, after a few kilometres running straight as a die, the narrow road is back among huge rock formations, which must be circumvented. One, two serpentine sweeps upwards into the rock. Far below, the secluded bays emerge along the cape. Then the road cuts into the stone, scampering beneath the mountain towards the next viewing level then delivering a sudden burst of déjà-vu. It's a bit like the famous US coast road, Highway Number One. A pocket version of the Pacific Coast Highway on Majorca. What a thing!

We continue onwards. The outermost end of northern Majorca is ragged and proud, carved from barren rock. It's single narrow road leads twisting and turning to the very end – as far as the lighthouse on Cap de Formentor. Standing in the Mediterranean wind, blinking in the sunlight, comes the chilling realisation that we've perhaps just completed the first half of our Majorca tour.

RESTAURANT

EL SOL
PUIG DE BONANY
07549 SON SERRA DE MARINA
WWW.SUNSHINE-BAR.NET

ERMITA DE LA
VICTORIA

CALA MESQUIDA

bis ganz ans Ende. Bis zum Leuchtturm am Kap de Formentor. Dort wird uns in die Sonne blinzelnd und im Wind des Mittelmeers fröstelnd klar, dass wir die Halbzeit unserer Mallorca-Runde vielleicht gerade überschritten haben. Die Berge der Tramuntana liegen hinter uns, was soll nun noch kommen? – Beinahe benommen geht es zurück ins Auto und dann fassen wir einen Entschluss: Mallorca hat uns bereits so viel gegeben, da werden wir auch den Rest aufmerksam genießen. Wenn wir in den letzten Tagen eines über diese Insel gelernt haben, dann, dass sie immer für eine Überraschung gut ist. Zuerst aber: gut gelaunt und wie Könige zurück nach Port de Pollença. Und dieses Mal nehmen wir sogar

The mountains of Tramuntana lie behind us, so what's next? We return to the car almost dazed and then reach a decision: Majorca has already given us so much, so we'll be sure to enjoy the rest, too. If we've learnt one thing about this island over the last few days, it's that it's full of surprises. But first we head back to Port de Pollenca in high spirits and feeling like kings. This time we even take in the promenade, inhaling the inimitably fragrant mixture of city and sea, allowing ourselves to be ogled by tourists sporting flip-flops and sunglasses, being overcome by the utterly mundane urge to spend some time on the beach. Bum-bum Latin disco beat – the final bars of some summer hit, something to do with Corazón.

die Uferpromenade mit. Inhalieren den unnachahmlichen Duft der Mischung von Stadt und Meer, lassen uns von badelatschenden, sonnenbebrillten Touristen begaffen, bekommen ganz irdische Lust auf eine Auszeit am Strand. Bumm-Bumm-Latin-Disco-Beat. Letzte Reste irgendeines Sommer-Hits, irgendwas mit Corazón. Dazu ein Cafè auf den Stühlen vorn an der Straße. Aber das hält nicht lang. Wir wollen ganz schnell weiter und flitzen auf der Küstenstraße in Richtung Süden, wechseln dann bei Alcúdia in die nächste Bucht – eine Besichtigung der gotischen Kirche Sant Jaume und des alten römischen Theaters dort schreiben wir auf die To-Do-List fürs nächste Mal. Dass wir wiederkommen, ist nämlich jetzt schon sonnenklar. Vorbei an Can Picafort, auf der Ma-12 nach Osten, das Land ist flach und weit. Hinter alten Steinmauern am Straßenrand breiten sich karge Felder und wuchernde Gärten aus. Dann drängen sich erneut niedrige Hügelkuppen heran und lassen die Straße ansteigen, wieder abfallen: Gefühlt schnurgerade strebt das Asphaltband in der warmen Nachmittagssonne dahin, hinter uns gleißt die Straße wie ein Band aus Silber. Bald taucht die burgähnliche Wallfahrtskirche Sant Salvador über dem Städtchen Artà auf, jetzt haben wir es beinahe bis ganz in den Osten der Insel geschafft. Erst am kleinen Flecken Canyamel ist die Reise zu Ende, wenige Meter noch huscht die Straße in den Felsen der Bucht entlang und landet dann in einer Sackgasse unterhalb überhängender Felswände.

Hier liegt der Eingang zu den Coves d'Artà einem riesigen Tropfsteinhöhlensystem, das am frühen Abend beinahe verwaist ist. Während der Hochsaison kann ein Besuch Klaustrophobie auslösen – jetzt, kurz vor Ende der Öffnungszeit, schlendern nur wenige Besucher andächtig durch die Hallen. Wir sind die Letzten auf der langen Treppe zurück ins Freie. Draußen ist es Abend geworden, Sonnenstrahlen blitzen durch die Silhouetten der Pinienbäume und lassen die Wellen unten in der Bucht glitzern. Ein warmer Wind sickert die Hänge herab und verführt zu offenen Seitenscheiben. In Porto Cristo, knapp 30 Kilometer später, ist die Sonne nur noch Erinnerung. Gute Nacht, Mallorca, wie schön du doch bist.

Dann drängen sich erneut niedrige Hügelkuppen heran und lassen die Straße ansteigen, wieder abfallen: Gefühlt schnurgerade strebt das Asphaltband in der warmen Nachmittagssonne dahin, hinter uns gleißt die Straße wie ein Band aus Silber.

Then low hill crests start pushing their way towards us, causing the road to start rising and falling. The strip of asphalt seems to be making a beeline into the warm afternoon sun, with the road glistening behind us like a band of silver.

Throw in a cup of coffee seated on the chairs out on the pavement. But it doesn't last long. We want to press on and dart along the coast road heading south, reaching the next bay at Alcúdia. We add a visit to the gothic church of Sant Jaume and the old Roman theatre to our to-do list for next time. A return visit is already a no-brainer. We pass Can Picafort on the Ma-12 heading east. The land is flat and expansive. Spread out behind old stone walls along the roadside are bare fields and sprawling gardens. Then low hill crests start pushing their way towards us, causing the road to start rising and falling. The strip of asphalt seems to be making a beeline into the warm afternoon sun, with the road glistening behind us like a band of silver. The fortress-like pilgrimage church of Sant Salvador emerges above the small town of Artà. We're now almost as the easternmost tip of the island. The end of the road is the tiny resort of Canyamel, where it scurries for a few metres further into the rocks along the bay, coming to a dead end in the shadow of overhanging rock faces. This marks the entrance to the Coves d' Artà, a huge cave system filled with stalagmites and stalactites, which is virtually deserted in the early evening. During busy times, a visit here can be positively claustrophobic, but now, shortly before closing time, only a few visitors are wandering agog through its innards. We're the last on the long staircase back into the open. Outside, it's now evening. The sun glints around the silhouettes of the pine trees and makes the waves shimmer on the bay down below. In Porto Cristo, almost 30 kilometres later, the sun is but a memory. Goodnight Majorca. How lovely you are.

HOTEL & RESTAURANT

PREDI SON JAUMELL
CARRETERA CALA MESQUIDA
CAPDEPERA
TEL: +34 971 818796
WWW.HOTELSONJAUMELL.COM

SON GENER
CARRETERA VIEJA SON SERVERA
SON SERVERA
TEL: +34 971 183612
WWW.SONGENER.COM

LLUC PORTO CRISTO

Nachdem uns die Serra de Tramuntana für die ersten beiden Tagesetappen intensiv begleitet hat, lassen wir das Gebirge im Westen Mallorcas auf der dritten Etappe endgültig hinter uns. Der Ausklang dieser großartigen Landschaft kann allerdings gebührend gefeiert werden: Mit den Kilometern zum Kap Formentor am nördlichsten Zipfel der Insel liegt noch einmal ein höchst intensiver und landschaftlich reizvoller Streckenabschnitt vor uns, der – hin und zurück – gleich zweimal absolviert werden muss. Von hier aus rollen wir in die nördlichen Ausläufer der großen, zentralen Ebene Mallorcas hinein, halten uns stets an der Küste und landen zum Ende der Etappe in den Bergen der Serres de Llevant. Die sind zwar nicht so hoch und rau wie das Tramuntana-Gegenstück, haben aber ihren ganz eigenen, milden Reiz. Schluss der Etappe ist nach einem Besuch der Tropfsteinhöhle von Artà beim Städtchen Porto Cristo, etwas nördlicher der hier gelegenen Drachen-Höhlen „Coves del Drac".

—

After the intense companionship of the Serra de Tramuntana on the first two days, we finally leave the mountain range on the west side of Majorca behind us on the third stage. The finale delivered by this fantastic landscape is nevertheless a fitting celebration. The kilometres to Cap de Formentor on the northernmost tip of the island offer yet another intense and scenically stunning piece of road, which – there and back – simply has to be covered twice. From here, we roll into the northern foothills of Majorca's great central plain, sticking resolutely to the coast and ultimately completing the stage in the mountains of the Serres de Llevant. They may not be quite as high and rugged as their Tramuntana counterparts, but nevertheless have their own, gentler appeal. Following a visit to the Caves of Artà, we reach the end of the stage at the small town of Porto Cristo, a little north of the "Coves del Drac" (Dragon Caves).

193 KM • 5,5 STUNDEN // 119 MILES • 5,5 HOURS

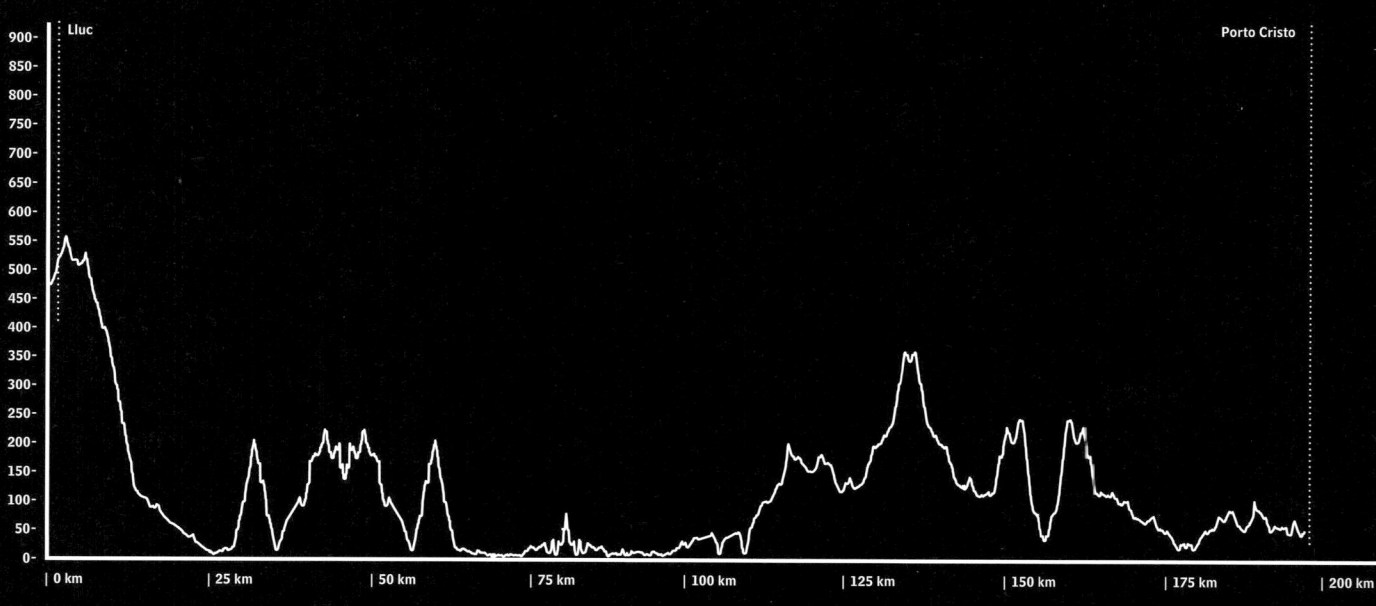

PORTO CRISTO
PALMA DE MALLORCA

147 KM • 3 STUNDEN // 92 MILES • 3 HOURS

Der Blick aus dem Fenster verheißt nichts Gutes: Keine Berge weit und breit. Porto Cristo fläzt sich an die Ostküste Mallorcas, fühlt sich heute schon am Morgen an wie eine immerwährende Siesta unter in Seebrise flatternden Sonnenschirmen. Für einen Moment kämpfen wir mit akuter Urlaubs-Paralyse, diesem gähnenden Gefühl von Antriebslosigkeit angesichts der Prognose „gutes Buch und ab auf die Liege".

—

The view from the window is not particularly promising – not a mountain in sight far and wide. Porto Cristo sits slouched on Majorca's east coast, and today, even first thing in the morning, there's a feeling of perpetual siesta beneath parasols fluttering in the sea breeze. For a brief moment, we battle with acute holiday paralysis – this yawning feeling of listlessness accompanied by a prognosis of "stretch out on the sun lounger with a good book".

Dann siegt die innere Unruhe. Wäre doch gelacht, wenn es auf den Kilometern zurück nach Palma nichts zu entdecken gäbe. Und: Fahrfreude ist, was man daraus macht. Deshalb rein ins Auto, aufmachen für die Sonne, vielleicht sogar statt Motorsound ein wenig „Big Red Machine": Vocoder-Falsetto und DX7-Licks räkeln sich hier für uns mit verschmiertem Lippenstift auf perlenden Hypnose-Gitarren-Samples, ein Barpiano scheppert in einer Katzenfutterdose durch eine Sonntagnachmittagsdepression, feierliche Gospelorgel-Schmuser landen mit Glitzergirlanden und Heavy-Metal-Riffs umhängt klirrend im Sequenz-Häcksler – aber hey, Donna Summer ginge jetzt definitiv auch. Abba? – Und ob! Frank Sinatra? – Klar doch! Johnny Cash oder Metallica? – Ein wenig düster vielleicht, aber wenn das die individuelle Vorstellung von Gute-Laune-Musik trifft, ganz selbstverständlich: Ja. Oder, um es mit Leonard Cohen zu sagen: Hallelujah.

Für mehr als einen Song reicht die erste Etappe ohnehin nicht, wir schaffen es kaum bis in den vierten Gang, denn bereits am südlichen Ende von Porto Cristo haben wir den nächsten Tropfsteinhöhlen-Ortstermin. Die Coves del Drac mit ihren beleuchteten unterirdischen Sälen sind eine andere Welt, in die es sich zu verschwinden lohnt, und gegen das knisternde Vergnügen, unter Tage eine Bootsfahrt zu unternehmen, lässt sich sowieso nichts einwenden. Der Rückweg ins Freie ist danach ähnlich wie am Abend vorher an der Höhle von Artà wunderbar beruhigend. Von drinnen nach draußen, von dunkel nach hell, und irgendwie beginnt man sich spätestens jetzt zu fragen, ob sich an diesem Teil der Küste wohl noch mehr ähnliche Höhlen und Klüfte verbergen. Ein paar Schritte weiter im Landesinneren, auf der betriebsamen Ringstraße, ist davon nichts zu sehen, aber vorne am Meer besteht die Costa de Llevant aus unzähligen kleinen und großen Buchten, die an kleinen Stränden oder unter Felsen und Rissen enden. Dies wäre Material für eine Tour auf der Vespa: durchs Land stromern, sich dann an kleinen und kleinsten Wegen zum Meer durchschlagen und so den Sommer mit salziger Haut und feuchter Badehose genießen. Aber das gilt für einen anderen Tag.

But the inner restlessness wins through. We would laugh if it turns out there's nothing to see on the kilometres back to Palma. And the joy of driving is what you make of it. So, it's back into the car, top down for the sun, perhaps even a bit of "Big Red Machine" instead of rich engine sound – vocoder falsetto and DX7 licks loll around with smeared lipstick on sparkling, hypnotic guitar samples; a lounge piano rattles inside a cat-food tin through a Sunday afternoon depression; the embracing sound of uplifting gospel organ lands clanking in the sequence shredder bedecked with glittering garlands and heavy-metal riffs. But hey – Donna Summer would also work right now. Abba? – absolutely! Frank Sinatra? – of course! Johnny Cash or Metallica? – a little morose maybe, but if that fits with your individual idea of good-mood music then, obviously, yes. Or, to say it with Leonard Cohen – hallelujah.

In any event, the first stretch doesn't last more than one song. We've barely made it into fourth gear and we're already at our next date with a dramatic cave formation on the southern edge of Porto Cristo. The Coves del Drac, with their illuminated subterranean caverns are another world into which it is definitely worth disappearing. And there's nothing to be said against the tantalizing pleasure of an underground boat trip. Much like the evening before at the Caves of Artà, the return to the open afterwards is wonderfully calming. From inside to outside, from darkness to light, and somehow you start to ask yourself whether there are more of these caves and chasms hidden along this coast. A few steps farther inland, on the bustling ring road, there's no sign of this at all. But along the shore, the Costa de Llevant is made up of countless bays, large and small, that end on small beaches or beneath rocks and crevices. This would be good material for a tour on a Vespa – roaming through the countryside, pushing onward along ever smaller roads and tracks, enjoying the summer with salty skin and wet swimming shorts.

But that's something for another day. We obviously haven't lost sight of our stated aim of doing a full lap of the island, despite initial hesitation. We take a right at

Wir haben unser Ziel einer Inselrunde trotz anfänglichem Zögern natürlich nicht aus den Augen verloren. Bei Portocolom biegen wir nach rechts ab, surfen ins Landesinnere und nehmen dann vor Felanitx den Abzweig zum Puig de Sant Salvador. Ein Insulaner hat uns auf die Idee gebracht. Es sei auf Mallorca ein wahrer Geheimtipp, die vielen Einsiedeleien zu besuchen, die das tiefreligiöse Land zu bieten hat. Und irgendwo muss man eben beginnen. Deshalb: tapfer die Kurven bergauf nehmen und dann tatsächlich staunen. Der Ausblick vom Santuario, dem kleinen Turm-Monument am Gipfel, ist wunderschön. Wie struppige, grüne Riesenköpfe schlafen die Hügel ringsum, in der Ferne liegt Dunst über dem Meer. Das war so schön, dass wir es ein paar Kilometer weiter gleich noch einmal versuchen: Einmal den Haken nach Felanitx schlagen, dann auf der Ma-14 zurück nach Südosten in die Hügel hineinfahren und das Castell de Santueri besuchen. Von den alten Zinnen der Festung kann man hinüberwinken zum Puig de Sant Salvador und sich bei einem kurzen Abenteuer-Spaziergang in der Macchia verirren. Spätestens jetzt haben wir uns mit dem flachen Südosten der Insel angefreundet und erleben, dass nach den fokussierten Bergetappen der vorherigen Tage das entspannte Reisetempo des heutigen Tages ganz gut ins Programm passt.

In Santanyí angekommen grummelt der Magen. Wir finden das „East 26", fliegen innerhalb einer knappen Stunde kulinarisch einmal rund um die Welt und sind fassungslos: Es scheint auf Mallorca Gesetz zu werden, dass hier gut gegessen werden kann. Mit dem Tellerabräumen kommt uns eine Idee: Auf einer Landkarten-Rückseite sammeln wir die besten Ess-Momente der letzten Tage – zu gut, um sie zu vergessen. Da war gleich zu Beginn die Tranche von Spanferkel in Estellencs. Danach gegrillten Fisch in Deià, schwitzend in der Sonne sitzend, das säuerliche Aroma von Seetang und Salz in der Nase. In Porto Pollença gab es den Koch aus – Moment mal – Argentinien? Chile? Venezuela? Uruguay? – Egal, das Essen war traumhaft. Dann das Ca na Toneta in Caimari. Eine Welt für sich. Und jetzt eben gegrillter Tintenfisch. Wir strahlen uns über den Tisch an, streicheln imaginäre

Ein Insulaner hat uns auf die Idee gebracht. Es sei auf Mallorca ein wahrer Geheimtipp, die vielen Einsiedeleien zu besuchen, die das tiefreligiöse Land zu bieten hat.

An islander gave us the idea. It's a real insider tip on Majorca to visit the many hermitages this deeply religious land has to offer.

Portocolom, surf inland and then, outside Felanitx, take the turning for Puig de Sant Salvador. An islander gave us the idea. It's a real insider tip on Majorca to visit the many hermitages this deeply religious land has to offer. And you have to start somewhere. So, we dutifully tackle the bends up the mountainside to then be utterly amazed. The view from Santuario, the small tower monument at the top, is absolutely stunning. The hills round about look like the shaggy, green heads of sleeping giants. In the distance, a fine haze hangs above the sea. It was so beautiful that we try again a few kilometres further on – taking the turning for Felanitx then driving back into the hills towards the southeast on the Ma-14 to visit the Castell de Santueri. From the battlements of the ancient fortress, you can wave over to the Puig de Sant Salvador and then get lost during a short but adventurous walk through the undergrowth. By now, we've warmed to the flat southeast of the island and discover that, following the concentrated mountain stages of the previous days, the relaxed pace of this day actually fits into the programme very well.

Our stomachs are rumbling by the time we reach Santanyí. We find the "East 26" and, in the space of an hour, make a culinary journey around the world that leaves us speechless. Eating well seems to be the law here on Majorca. As the plates are cleared away, an idea occurs to us: We cobble together the best eating moments of the last few days on the back of a map – too good to forget. It started with the portion of suckling pig in Estellencs, followed by grilled fish in Deià as we sat sweating in the sun, the acidic aroma of seaweed and salt in our noses. In Porto Pollenca, the chef was from – wait a minute – Argentina? Chile? Venezuela? Uruguay? – wherever, the food was fantastic. Then there was the Ca na Toneta

RESTAURANTS

EAST 26
CARRER DEL BISBE VERGER, 26
SANTANYÍ
TEL: +34 871 03 18 38
WWW. EAST26-MALLORCA.COM

TOMATES VERDES RESTAURANT,
CARRER DE LA CONSTITUCIÓ, 2,
07620 LLUCMAJOR

WWW.TOMATESVERDES.COM

FINCA

FINCA SON RISA
RANDA
WWW.LUXURY-HIDEAWAY.COM

WWW.FINCASERVICE.DE
WWW.LANDMARK-FINE-TRAVEL.DE
WWW.MALLORCA-FINCAVERMIETUNG.COM

Bäuche und schmatzen in seliger Erinnerung. Irgendwann kommt dann aber doch, was kommen muss, die Landkarte dreht sich und ein Zeigefinger geht suchend auf die Reise: „Wir sind … hier!" Trigger-Satz aller Reisesüchtigen und Fernwehkranken. Bis ans Meer bei Sant Jordi muss es schon noch gehen, das ist klar, sonst hätten wir die Küste nicht in ihrer Gänze abgefahren, und das ist Ehrensache. „Auf der Küstenstraße runter nach Palma langweilen, geht ja gar nicht, es muss doch eine schöne Alternative geben", ist allerdings bereits der nächste Satz, und jetzt fallen begehrliche Blicke auf die Höhenlinien im Inneren der Insel. „Puig de Randa, würde ich sagen." – „Campos, Llucmajor, dann sieht man was von Land und Leuten, ab dann hast du recht." Wie einig wir uns immer sind …

Auf unserem Weg nach dem Motto „immer der Nase nach" stellen wir zweierlei fest: Erstens, Mallorca hat auch fade Seiten. Zweitens liegt das nur daran, dass die anderen Ecken so traumhaft schön sind. Ein paar Kilometer geradeaus mit Feldern und Ackerland links und rechts kann man da schon mal mitnehmen. Vor allem, weil die Fahrt auf den Tafelberg Puig de Randa mit seinen Doppelhügeln und dem majestätischen Rundumblick die Reise wirklich lohnt. Die Landschaft erinnert an abgelegene Zipfel der Pyrenäen, an den schläfrigen Rand der italienischen Alpen kurz vor der Po-Ebene, als würde sich die Gegend in vollkommene Weltfremdheit zurückziehen, um Ruhe vor dem Lärm der Ebene zu haben. Das Bodenpersonal folgt diesem Ruf ganz augenscheinlich besonders gern. Auf das Santuari de Nostra Senyora de Gràcia und die Ermita de Sant Honorat folgt ein paar Serpentinen später das Santuari de Nostra Senyora de Cura – für Agnostiker und Atheisten oder auch nur Protestanten wird es da schon unübersichtlich, welches Heiligtum, Kloster, Einsiedelei denn nun welchem Zweck dient. Man darf das mangels Insider-Wissen aber auch unkommentiert lassen. Es ist schließlich so: Zwischen den Fahrern verschiedener Sportwagenfabrikate soll es auf der Ideallinie und an Ampeln immer wieder zu tumultartigen Szenen kommen, dabei will am Ende doch

in Caimari. In a world of its own. And now, grilled squid. We beam at one another across the table, stroking imaginary bellies and smacking our lips in blissful remembrance.

Eventually, however, what must happen, happens. We turn the map back over and an index finger wanders the page: "We're … here!" The trigger phrase for all travel addicts and those suffering from wanderlust. It's apparent that we have to head for the sea at Sant Jordi, otherwise we won't have driven the entire coast – and that's a matter of honour. However, the next sentence is: "There's no way we're following the tedious coast road down to Palma. There must be a good alternative." And covetous eyes are drawn to the contours in the island's interior. "Puig de Randa, I would say." – "Campos, Llucmajor, then we see something of the land and the people. After that, you're right enough." We're always in agreement … Travelling to the principle of "always follow your nose", two things are apparent to us: First, Majorca also has bland sides. Second, that's only because the other parts are so stunningly gorgeous. You have to accept a few straight kilometres flanked by fields and farmland. Especially because the drive to the flat-topped Puig de Randa, with its twin peaks and its majestic 360-degree vista is truly worthwhile. The landscape is evocative of the remote peaks of the Pyrenees, of the sleepy edges of the Italian Alps just before the flood plains of the River Po, as if it would withdraw into total unworldliness to escape the noise and clamour of the plains. The locals are apparently very keen to live up to this reputation. The Santuari de Nostra Senyora de Gràcia and the Ermita de Sant Honorat are followed a couple of serpentines later by the Santuari de Nostra Senyora de Cura – for agnostics and atheists and even protestants, it quickly becomes impossible to tell which sanctuary, monastery, hermitage serves which purpose. There's no need to discuss the lack of insider knowledge. Here's what it is: The drivers of different sports-car manufacturers are repeatedly involved in tumultuous scenes on the ideal line and at traffic lights. Yet, at the end of the day, they are all merely

PLATJA DES TRENC

CASTELL DE SANTUERI

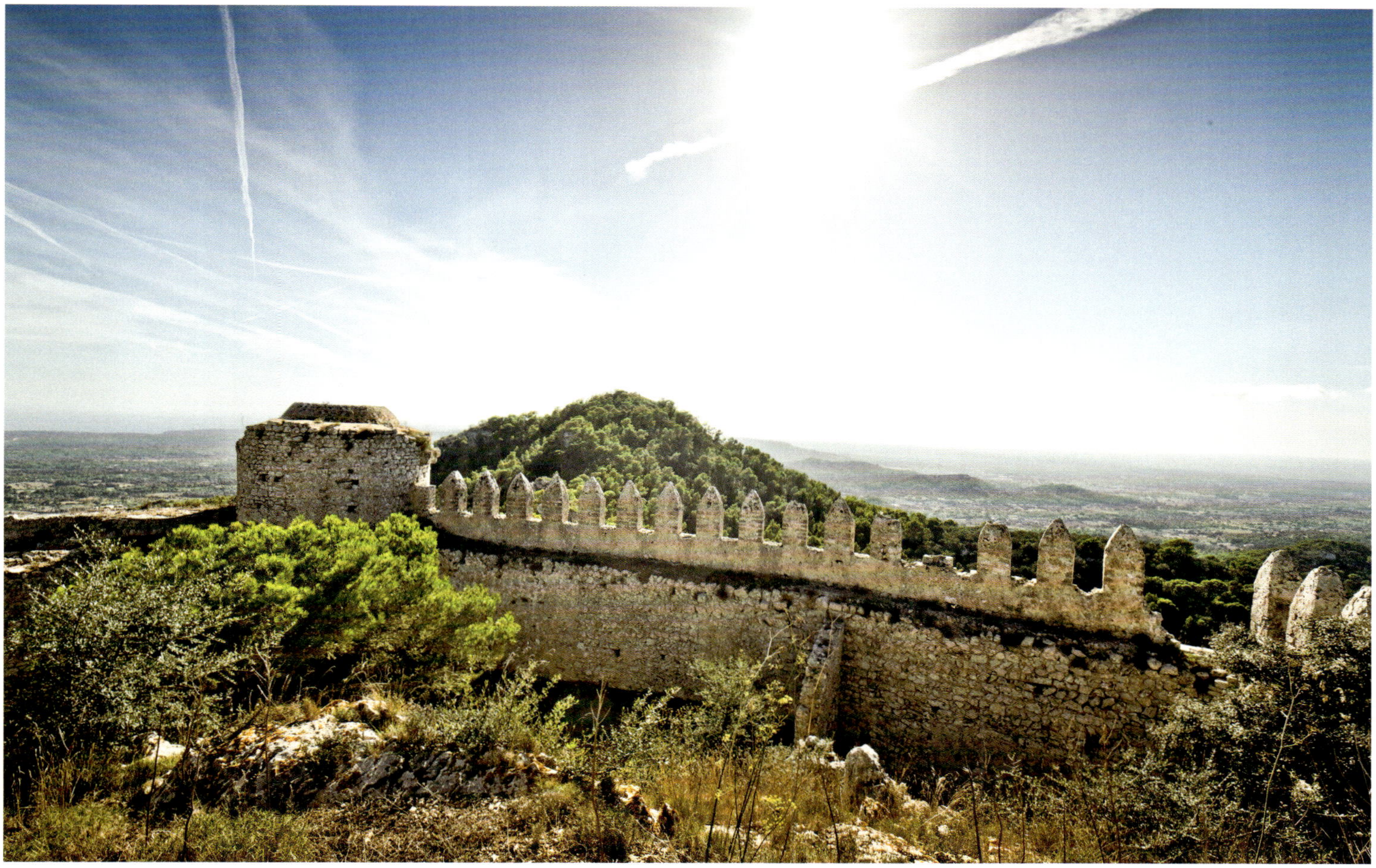
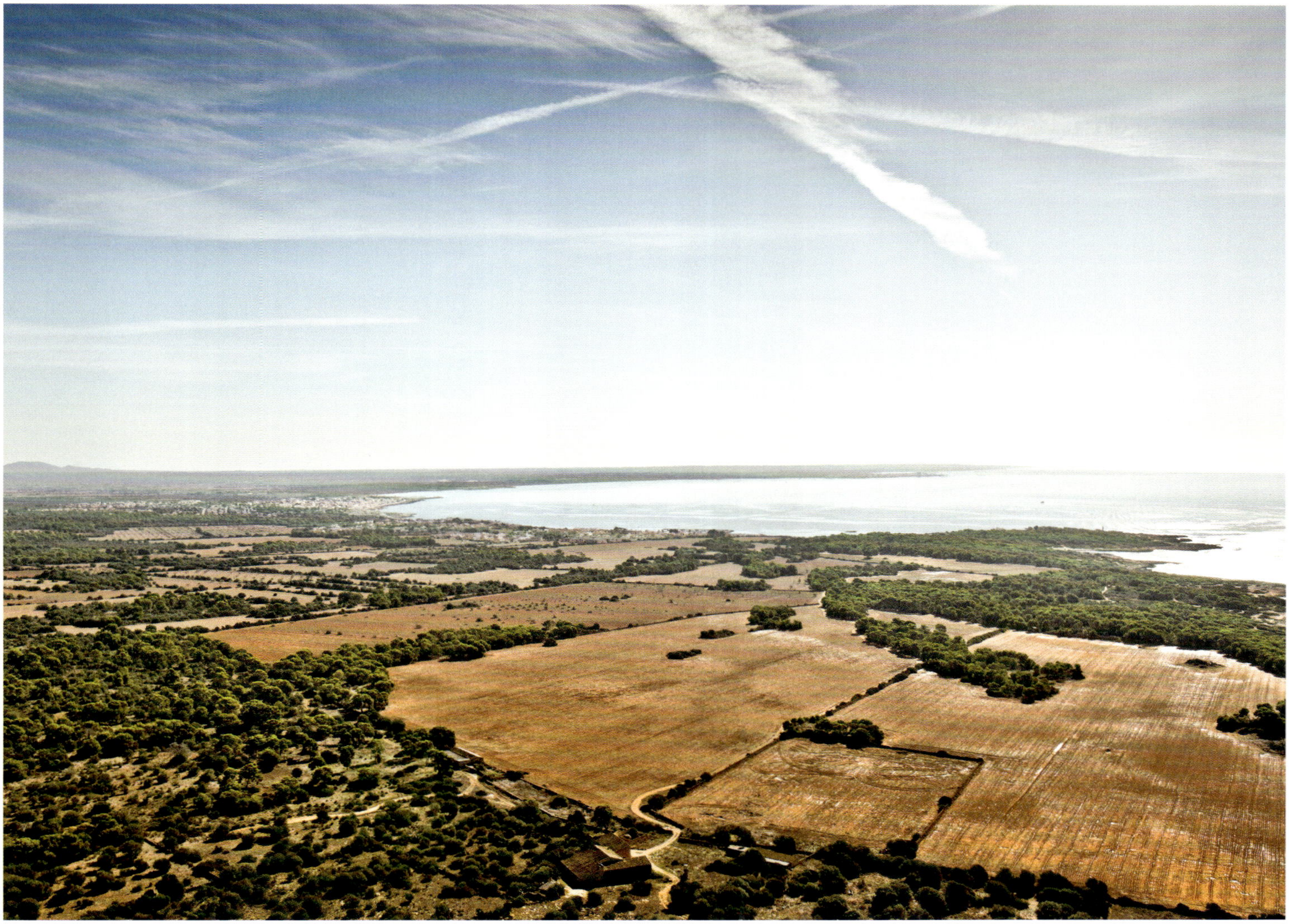

einfach nur jeder in den Fahrfreude-Himmel. Für Außenstehende mag der Unterschied zwischen Flat-Six und 180-Grad-V8 marginal sein, für Insider ist er aber faktisch heilsentscheidend. Wir fühlen uns den frommen Bewohnern des Berges so gesehen auf alle Fälle tief verbunden. Strömen dann andächtig zurück ins Tal, über Algaida und Pina weiter nach Norden und machen erst in Sineu Halt. Exakt die Mitte der Insel. Das musste sein. Und jetzt: Palma de Mallorca. 30 Kilometer Luftlinie, eine starke halbe Stunde Fahrt. So klein kann Mallorca sein.

30 Minuten reichen aber, um die letzten Tage noch einmal sacken zu lassen. Die Insel in ihrer ganzen, derben Schönheit. Ein gutes Gefühl. Dann schluckt uns Palma mit Verkehrsstaus, Lärm und Menschenmengen. Langsam kriechen wir hinunter zum Hafen. Alle Zeit der Welt. Gänsehaut beim Anblick von La Seu. Dann der Hafen. Die Fähre zurück nach Barcelona wartet schon. Wir zucken mit den Schultern und drehen ab. Mit dieser Insel sind wir noch lange nicht fertig. Gerade erst geht alles los.

seeking entry into the heaven of driving joy. For outsiders, the difference between a flat six and a 180-degree V8 may be marginal. But for insiders it is, in fact, crucial to salvation. In this respect, we feel a truly deep bond with the mountain's pious inhabitants and wend our way devoutly back down into the valley, continuing north via Algaida and Pina, not stopping until we reach Sineu. Right in the centre of the island. It had to be. And now – Palma de Mallorca. 30 kilometres as the crow flies. Half an hour of steady driving. That's how small Majorca can be.

However, 30 minutes are enough to allow the last few days to sink in. The island in all its earthy glory. It's a good feeling. Then Palma swallows us whole with its traffic jams, noise and heaving masses. Slowly we crawl down to the harbour. All the time in the world. Goose bumps when we look at La Seu. Then the harbour. The ferry back to Barcelona is already waiting. We shrug our shoulders and turn away. There's no way we're finished with this island. It's only just beginning.

RANDA

PORTO CRISTO PALMA DE MALLORCA

Die vierte und letzte Etappe einer Mallorca-Umrundung führt über die Hügel-Landschaft der Region Llevant im Nordosten, entlang des Meers im Osten mit seinen Tropfsteinhöhlen und der zerklüfteten Küste, danach bleibt der Rückweg zur Inselhauptstadt Palma durch die flachen Ausläufer der zentralen Ebene. Verglichen mit der spektakulären und rauen Gebirgslandschaft im Westen scheint diese Etappe deutlich abzufallen, kann aber trotzdem ihre Reize entfalten. Wer sich Zeit für die kleinen Fischerdörfer, Klöster und Eremitagen in den Hügeln nimmt, entdeckt ein Mallorca mit reduzierter Geschwindigkeit und sehenswerten Ecken. Die Fahrt ins Landesinnere ist nicht nur wegen eines Abstechers zum zentral gelegenen Puig de Randa lohnenswert, sondern auch, um einen Eindruck vom Charakter der Zentralebene zu erhalten: Ohne die einsilbige Atmosphäre dieser Landschaft ist das Bild von Mallorca unvollständig, sie nimmt einen großen Teil der Inselfläche ein. Mallorca ist mehr als Tourismus und Freizeit – das wird in dieser landwirtschaftlich stark genutzten Gegend zum Anfassen deutlich. Ein ehrliches Land.

—

The fourth and final stage of a tour around Majorca takes us over the hilly landscape of the Llevant region in the northeast, along the sea in the east, with its caves and rugged coastline. After that comes the road back to the island's capital, Palma, through the low foothills of the central plain. Compared with the spectacular and rugged mountain landscape in the west, this section seems like quite a come-down, but is nevertheless able to reveal its own appeal. If you take time to explore the little fishing villages, monasteries and hermitages in the hills, you discover a low-speed Majorca and plenty of corners worth seeing. The drive to the middle of the island is worthwhile not only for a detour to the central Puig de Randa but also to gain a feel for the character of the central plain. Without the monosyllabic atmosphere of this landscape, the image of Majorca is incomplete. It occupies a large proportion of the island's surface. Majorca is more than tourism and leisure – something that becomes patently obvious in this heavily agricultural region. A simple, honest land.

147 KM • 3 STUNDEN // 92 MILES • 3 HOURS

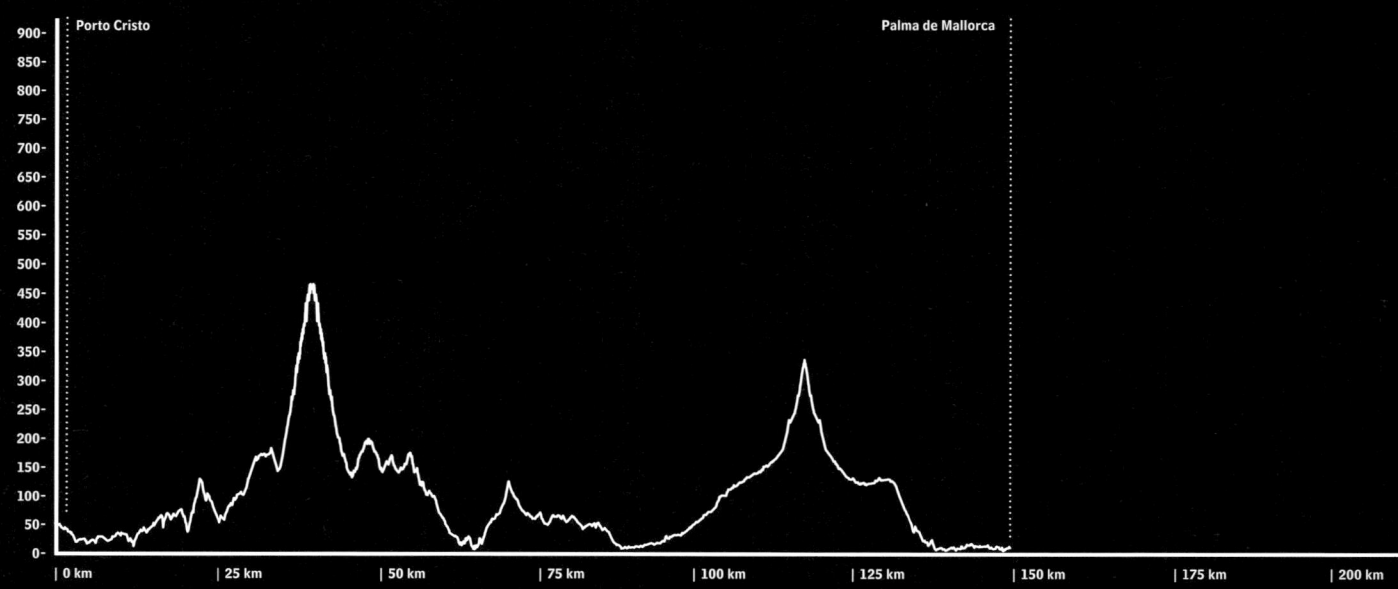

ASK A LOCAL

Toni Dezcallar ist ein Einheimischer, wie er im Buche steht. Nicht nur reichen die Wurzeln seiner Familie bis ins Mittelalter, er kennt außerdem auch jeden Stein auf der Insel. Und jede Kurve, was ihn für uns schon fast zum Inselheiligen macht. Vielleicht sollte man noch erwähnen, dass er Organisator der „Rallye Clásico Isla Mallorca" ist, eines ziemlich exklusiven Motorsport-Events mit traumhaften Rahmenbedingungen. Vielleicht lassen wir ihn aber auch lieber mal selbst sprechen.

—

Toni Dezcallar is the archetypal local. Not only do his family roots extend back to the Middle Ages, he also knows every rock on the island. And every curve – which, for us, pretty much makes him the island's patron saint. Perhaps we should also mention that he is the organiser of the "Rallye Clásico Isla Mallorca", a rather exclusive motorsport event with a fabulous set-up. Perhaps we should just let him explain it himself.

Hallo Toni! Kannst du mir etwas über dich erzählen? Mein Name ist Toni Dezcallar und ich gehöre zu einer Familie, die sich 1239 auf dieser Insel niedergelassen hat, also vor rund 800 Jahren. Im 13. Jahrhundert wurde uns ein Adelstitel verliehen, als der König von Aragon auf Mallorca lebte, und seitdem sind wir sehr stark mit dieser Insel verbunden. Meine Leidenschaft sind Autos, und seit ich klein war, habe ich in Autos geschlafen, bin tausende Kilometer ununterbrochen mit dem Auto gefahren und bin als Amateur auch Kart gefahren. Als ich nach meinem Universitätsabschluss in Heidelberg aus Deutschland zurückkam, sah ich im Jahr 2003 hier auf Mallorca eine Oldtimer-Rallye und entschied, dass ich mitmachen wollte: Genau das wollte ich machen. Also habe ich in diesem Sommer einen Seat 124 Coupé gekauft, wir haben das ganze Jahr an ihm

Hi Toni! Can you tell me a little about yourself? My name is Toni Dezcallar and I belong to a family that has been established on this island since 1239, that's around 800 years. We got a nobility title back in the 1300s when the King of Aragon lived on Mallorca and since then we've been very strongly connected to this island. My passion is cars and since I was very little I have been sleeping in cars, driving a car non-stop for thousands of kilometres, and was karting as an amateur. When I came back from Germany, from my university degree in Heidelberg, I saw a classic car rally here in Mallorca in the year 2003 and I decided that I wanted to participate: this was exactly what I wanted to do. So that summer I bought a Seat 124 Coupé, we built it all year, and in 2004 I raced my first rally with my brother, which we finished –

geschraubt. 2004 bin ich mit meinem Bruder meine erste Rallye gefahren, die wir auch beendet haben – wir wissen nicht genau wie, aber wir haben es geschafft. Danach übernahm ich 2005 die Organisation der Rallye Clásico Isla Mallorca, die 2019 15 Jahre alt wird. Mit dieser Rallye habe ich eine Art Familie der Clásico Isla Mallorca gegründet, bestehend aus Deutschen, Briten und Österreichern, Belgiern, Schweizern, Franzosen, Spaniern, Italienern und Portugiesen. Wir haben eine internationale Veranstaltung geschaffen, bei der sich jeder mag. Nur nette Leute, die den unterhaltsamen Aspekt des Sports verstehen, immer mit Respekt für ihre Konkurrenten. Die Rallye dauert drei Tage und findet immer am zweiten Wochenende im März statt – Donnerstag, Freitag und Samstag. Am Donnerstag gibt es zwei Nachtetappen und am Freitag und am Samstag je sechs Etappen, die insgesamt etwa 150 Kilometer ergeben. Die Rallye gilt als eine der fünf besten Veranstaltungen auf der Insel und wird von der Polizei und von den Straßenbehörden bestens unterstützt. Die Straßen sind während der Rallye für den normalen Verkehr gesperrt, und wir sind die einzige Veranstaltung, für die das Cap de Formentor oder Sa Calobra geschlossen werden. Es gibt diese Etappe namens Col de Sa Crou – Col de Estords – das ist wie unsere Nordschleife, denn das ist eine richtige Rallye-Etappe, die kürzlich neu asphaltiert wurde. Der Asphalt ist neu, aber die Straße ist genau so, wie sie vor 40 oder 50 Jahren war. Sie beginnt in Caserna, von der Militärbasis aus.

Wo ist der Hauptsitz? Gibt es verschiedene Kategorien? Der Hauptsitz ist in Puerto Portals, das ist auch einer der Sponsoren. Wir beginnen zwischen 8:30 und 9 Uhr morgens, aber wir versuchen, zwischen 17 und 18 Uhr nachmittags im Ziel zu sein, damit die Leute sich ein bis zwei Stunden lang entspannen können, bevor sie zum Abendessen gehen. Es ist eine Kombination aus Lifestyle und Motorsport, und wir schaffen es wirklich sehr gut, dieses Gleichgewicht zu finden. Wir haben zwei Kategorien: Gleichmäßigkeit und Wettbewerb. In der Regel kann jeder mit einem vor 1981 gebauten Auto an der Rallye teilnehmen. Man benötigt nur zwei Helme und einen Feuerlöscher. Im Wettbewerb haben wir Autos bis zur Gruppe 4: Mit diesen Autos kann man die Rallye offiziell gewinnen. Wir haben jetzt auch eine Youngtimer-Klasse bis 1990 mit separater Wertung aufgemacht. Du kannst mit einem BMW M3, einem Porsche 911, einem Ford Sierra Cosworth, einem Subaru Legacy oder einem Toyota Celica ST 165 der Gruppe A teilnehmen. Wir passen uns also langsam an die Bedürfnisse neuer Kunden oder jüngerer Menschen an. Unser Limit liegt bei 95 Autos, weil Geld letztendlich nicht alles ist.

Was ist das Besondere an Mallorca? Und wenn Sie einen Freund besuchen würden, welchen Weg würden Sie nehmen, um ihm eine tolle Tour zu bieten? Das Fantastische an der Insel ist ihre Landschaft. Du kannst in Llubi fahren, das flach und gerade ist, und kannst eine Etappe wie den Col de Sa Creu fahren. Oder man fährt vom Null-

funnily enough, we don't even know how, but we finished. After that, I took over organising the the Rally Clásico Isla Mallorca in 2005, which in 2019 is going to turn 15. What I have achieved through this rally is to create a family of the Rally Clásico Isla Mallorca, of Germans, British, Austrians, Belgians, Swiss, French, Spanish, Italians, Portuguese. So we've created an international event at which everybody likes each other. Only nice people who understand the fun part of it, always with respect to their competitors.

The rally lasts three days. It is always held on the second weekend of March – Thursday, Friday and Saturday. We hold two night stages on Thursday, six stages on Friday and six stages on Saturday, which in total is around 150 kilometres. The rally is considered one of the top five events on the island. It's very much welcomed by the police and the road authorities. The roads are closed for normal traffic at the time we rally and we are the only event to close Cap de Formentor or Sa Calobra. There is this stage called Col de Sa Crou – Col de Estords – this is like our Nordschleife … because it's a proper rally stage and has been recently re-tarmacked, so the tarmac is new, but the road has remained exactly as it was 40 or 50 years ago. It's the one that starts from Caserna, from the military base.

Where is it based and do you have different categories? It's based in Puerto Portals, which is also one of the sponsors. We start at 8:30, 9 o'clock in the morning, but we try to finish at 5:00 to 6 o'clock in the afternoon so that people have time to relax for one or two hours before they go for dinner. It's a combination of lifestyle and motorsport, and we really manage to find that balance very well. We have two categories: regularity and competition. In regularity, anybody with a car built before 1981 can join the rally; they only need two helmets and one fire extinguisher. In competition, we have cars up to group four: these are the cars that can win the rally officially. But now we have opened a youngtimer section, where we open up to 1990. This has a separate classification. You can join with a BMW M3, Porsche 911, Ford Sierra Cosworth, a Subaru Legacy or a Toyota Celica ST 165 Group A. So we are slowly adapting to the needs of new customers or younger people. We set a limit of 95 cars, because in the end money is not everything.

What's so special about Mallorca and if you had a friend coming to visit you, which road would you take for a good ride? The fantastic thing about the island is its landscape. It enables you to drive in Llubi, which is flat and straight; and it enables you to go into a stage like Col de Sa Creu, or to go from a zero level to 700 metres which could be Puigmajor or it could be Sa Calobra. I would definitely drive the route from Cap de Formentor to Andratx. In the early morning, leave Palma at 6:30,

punkt auf 700 Meter, das könnte Puigmajor oder Sa Calobra sein. Ich würde definitiv die Strecke von Cap de Formentor nach Andratx fahren. Am frühen Morgen verlässt man Palma um 6:30 Uhr, um 7:30 Uhr ist man in Cap de Formentor und um 9 Uhr kann man in Andratx sein und frühstücken.

Welche Jahreszeit ist die beste? Oktober bis April.

Welcher Ort ist ein absolutes Muss für jeden Ausländer, der die Insel sehen möchte? Gibt es einen Ort ohne Tourismus, vielleicht ein nettes Restaurant oder einen schönen Strand? Nun, ich muss sagen, dass sich Mallorca in den letzten zehn Jahren enorm entwickelt hat. Bei Restaurants, Hotels und Dienstleistungen haben wir um 100 bis 200 Prozent zugelegt, wir haben hervorragende Arbeit geleistet. Die Restaurants, zu denen ich Leute schicken würde, sind Selva oder Miceli oder Santi Taura in Lloseta: Sie liefern immer 100 Prozent. Wenn ich einen Besucher auf eine Exkursion schicken müsste, würde ich empfehlen, alle Ermitas zu besuchen: Es gibt die Ermita de Betlém, die Ermita de la Victoria, die Ermita di San Miguel ... alle diese Ermitas sind auf Berggipfeln mit eine kleine Kirche oder einem spirituellen Ort, und die Straßen sind normalerweise fantastisch zu fahren. Aber ich werde die Leute auch immer nach Cap de Formentor und Sa Calobra schicken. Diese beiden Straßen sollte man unbedingt fahren.

Wie lange sollte jemand auf Mallorca und in Palma bleiben? Ich glaube es lohnt sich, ein oder zwei Tage nach Palma zu fahren. Die Stadt hat eine solche Atmosphäre, Orte wie Rosa oder Ramba oder diese fantastischen Restaurants, in denen man sein Mittag- oder Abendessen genießen kann. Aber es gibt so viel mehr als Palma, es gibt Mallorca: im Februar oder März durch die Oliven zu fahren, wenn die Mandelbäume rosa und weiß blühen, durch den Osten der Insel zu fahren, der völlig anders ist als der Westen. Da ist es zwar flacher, aber es ist eine sehr interessante Fahrt. Wenn man also eine Woche lang auf Mallorca ist, sollte man ein oder zwei Tage in Palma verbringen und die restlichen fünf Tage von Osten nach Westen fahren, durch Llucmajor im Süden und dann den ganzen Weg von Santanyí nach Port de Pollença. Du überquerst die gesamte Insel mit der Autobahn und am nächsten Tag kreuzt du den Weg erneut, einfach weiterfahren.

Lohnt es sich für ein oder zwei Tage ein Boot zu nehmen? Ja, sicher. Es ist wahrscheinlich kein Geheimnis, aber die Farben sind mit das Beste an Mallorca. Wenn man nach Mexiko reist oder sich die Orte an der Adriaküste ansieht, sind die wunderschön. Aber hier fährst du ungefähr fünf Minuten und findest eine Farbe, nach 30 Sekunden findest du eine andere und nach weiteren zwei Minuten findest du wieder eine andere. So geht das immer weiter. Man kann die Insel innerhalb von drei bis vier Tagen mit dem Boot umrunden und das ist ein einzigartiges Erlebnis. Mallorca vom Meer aus zu sehen ist unglaublich.

at 7:30 you are in Cap de Formentor, and at 9 o'clock you should be in Andratx, having breakfast.

What would be the best time of year? From October to April.

Which place is an insider must-see for any foreigner who wants to see the island, a non-tourist place, maybe a nice restaurant or a nice beach? Now I have to say over the last 10 years Mallorca has developed enormously, so service-wise, restaurants, hotels, I think we've increased by 100 percent to 200 percent, we've done a great, great job. The restaurants I would send you to are Selva, or Miceli, or Santi Taura in Lloseta: they always deliver 100 percent. If I had to send you on an excursion as a visitor, I would tell you to visit all the ermitas: you have the Ermita de Betlém, Ermita de la Victoria, Ermita di San Miguel ... all these Ermitas are on peaks of little mountains with a little church or a spiritual area, and the roads usually are fantastic to climb. But I will always send you to Cap de Formentor and Sa Calobra. So make sure you drive on those two roads.

How long should somebody stay in Mallorca and Palma? I think it's worth visiting Palma for one or two days. The city has created such an atmosphere, places like Rosa or Ramba or these fantastic restaurants where you can go and have lunch, dinner and enjoy. But there is so much more than Palma, there is Mallorca. To drive through the olives in February or March when the almond trees become pink and white, to drive through the east of the island which is completely different than the west, it's more flat but it's a very interesting drive. So, if you're in Mallorca for one week, drive around, spend one or two days in Palma, and the rest of the other five days drive from the east to the west and through Llucmajor in the south and then go all the way up from Santanyí to Port de Pollença, then you you cross the entire island with the motorway and the next day you cross it again, you keep driving.

Is it worth taking a boat for a day or two? Yes, for sure. It's probably not a secret but the colors are one of the biggest assets we have in Mallorca. When you go to Mexico, when you go to all the venues on the Adriatic coast, they are beautiful. But here you drive about five minutes and you find one and then you drive another 30 seconds to find another one and you drive or sail another two minutes and you find another one, and so on. You can basically do a round trip of the island in three or four days and it's also a unique experience. Seeing Mallorca from the sea – it's unbelievable.

www.rallyislamallorca.com

BAC KST AGE

Manchmal sieht man den Wald vor lauter Bäumen nicht: Mallorca, das ist ein Synonym für Sommerurlaub, Sonne und Party, beinahe schon für eine Art Kolonie des mediterranen Wohlseins. Mallorca, das kommt jedes Jahr irgendwie vorbei. Irgendwer im Freundes- und Bekanntenkreis fliegt immer gerade dorthin oder war gerade dort. Irgendwer hat immer einen brandheißen Geheimtipp für besonders entspannte, besonders preisgünstige Auszeit-Tage auf der Insel. Irgendwer ist immer im Frühjahrs-Rennrad-Trainingslager auf Mallorca. Für irgendwen gehören immer irgendwie zehn Tage Mallorca-All-Inclusive-Sommer zu einem gelungenen Jahr. Irgendwer schwört immer auf die ruhigen Nachsaison-Tage an der Küste Mallorcas. Irgendwer hat immer entfernte Bekannte, die sich gerade ein Haus in Santa Ponça oder eine Finca in Sollér gekauft haben, und irgendwer möchte immer irgendwen fragen, ob man dessen Ferienwohnung nicht auch einmal zum Freundschaftspreis … Irgendwelche Nachrichten berichten immer aus Mallorca, als ob die Insel gleich nebenan wäre. Irgendwie hat irgendwer immer irgendeine Meinung

Sometimes you can't see the wood for the trees. Majorca is synonymous with summer holiday, sun and party – almost a kind of colony of Mediterranean wellbeing. Majorca: it somehow comes around every year. Someone in your circle of friends and acquaintances is about to fly there or was just there. Someone always has a red-hot secret tip for a few super-relaxed days on the island at a bargain price. Someone is always at a spring racing-bike training camp on Majorca.

For some, ten days of all-inclusive Majorcan summer is a permanent fixture of a successful year. Someone always swears by the quiet off-season days on the coast of Majorca. Someone always has a distant acquaintance who has just bought themselves a house in Santa Ponça or a finca in Sollér. And someone always wants to ask someone else if they might offer special friends-and-family rates on their holiday apartment … Some news report or another is always reporting from Majorca, as if the island were right next door. Somehow, someone always has some

Danke an die Mallorquiner. Wir Mallorca-Fans muten Ihrer Insel manchmal einiges zu. Dass wir immer noch das Gefühl haben, von Herzen willkommen zu sein, das ist eine ganz spezielle Eigenschaft der Mallorquiner und vielleicht einer der größten Momente der Beliebtheit Ihrer Insel.

And now – thank you to the Mallorquins. Us fans of Majorca sometimes expect a lot from your island. That we still have the feeling of being warmly welcomed is a very special characteristic of the Mallorquins and perhaps one of the greatest moments of your island's popularity.

zu Mallorca. Als deshalb die Idee aufkam, CURVES nach Mallorca zu entführen, hat sich das zu Beginn, einen komischen Augenblick lang, angefühlt wie ein Scherz. Augenrollend abfälliger Satzbeginn: „Mallorca, das ist doch ...“ – und dann kamen die Adjektive in immer schnellerer Folge – „... eigentlich wunderschön. Manchmal atemberaubend. Ziemlich vielseitig. Ganz und gar nicht abgedroschen. Immer für eine Überraschung gut.“ Und so weiter.

Die beinahe absurde Idee von der Fahrt über die Lieblingsinsel aller Mitteleuropäer wurde mit diesem geschärften Fokus ganz schnell zu einem Lieblings-Unternehmen. Auf einmal war uns klar, dass diese Fahrt zu den Besten gehören könnte, die wir jemals unternommen haben. Wir wollten uns und der Insel beweisen, dass wir Mallorca richtig einschätzen. Vermutlich ging es auch allen Mitreisenden und Freunden im CURVES-Universum so, dass sie bei der ersten Erwähnung einer Runde über Mallorca im CURVES-Rhythmus große, ungläubige Augen bekommen haben. Um dann einen Gedanken später schon Feuer und Flamme zu sein. Für diese Begeisterungsfähigkeit und Neu-Entdeckungslust sagen wir Danke. Danke an Porsche, die zielsicher den famosen, kurvenscharfen, sperrangelweitoffenen Boxster GTS als ideales Fahrzeug für die Insel identifiziert und kurzerhand nach Palma de Mallorca verschifft haben. Samt kämpferischem Macan als Kamerafahrzeug und Gepäckschlucker mit Kurven-Talent. Wir fühlen uns verstanden. Ein exquisites Gefühl ist das. Danke an Freunde, Crew, Reisende, Mitdenker aus dem inneren CURVES-Kreis. Ihr wisst, wer ihr seid. Ohne euch würden wir nicht losfahren und nicht wiederkehren. Ihr macht die ganze Welt zur sehens- und lebenswerten Destination.

Danke aber auch an unsere Leser, die gerade jetzt ein CURVES in der Hand halten, mit dem Ziel Mallorca. Bestimmt haben auch Sie sich für eine Sekunde gefragt, „Weshalb Mallorca?" – und dann verstanden. So kennen wir Sie. Und jetzt kommt ein kleines Geständnis: Auch wenn wir immer behaupten CURVES nur für uns zu machen, wissen wir, dass

kind of opinion on Majorca. When this gave rise to the idea to whisk CURVES off to Majorca, it initially seemed, for a strange moment, like a joke. The eye-rolling derogatory sentence began: Majorca, but that's ..." – and then came the adjectives in increasingly rapid succession – "beautiful, actually. Sometimes breathtaking. Quite multifaceted. Not at all banal. Always good for a surprise." And so on.

With this sharpened focus, the almost absurd idea of the drive around every central European's favourite island quickly became a labour of love. It was suddenly clear to us that this drive could be one of the best we've ever done. We wanted to prove to ourselves and the island that we truly appreciate Majorca. All our travel companions and friends in the CURVES universe probably also widened their eyes in disbelief at the first mention of a tour of Majorca to the CURVES rhythm.

Then, having thought for a moment, found themselves brimming with enthusiasm for the idea. We thank you for this capacity for fervour and the desire to discover something new. Thank you to Porsche, which unerringly identified the excellent, corner-hugging, wide-open Boxster GTS as the ideal vehicle for the island and promptly shipped it to Palma de Mallorca, complete with the formidable Macan as camera vehicle, load-lugger and cornering meister. We feel understood – it's an exquisite sensation.

Thanks to friends, crew, travellers, like-minded souls from the inner CURVES circle. You know who you are. Without you, we would neither set off nor return. You make the whole world a destination worth seeing and experiencing. But thank you, too, to our readers – the people holding the Majorca issue of CURVES in their hands right now. You, too, probably thought for a second, "Why Majorca?" and then understood. We know how you tick. And now comes a small confession – although we always claim that we make CURVES only for ourselves,

das längst nicht mehr (immer) so ist. Wir machen CURVES auch für Sie. Weil wir uns auch von Ihnen verstanden fühlen. Und das ist ein ziemlich schöner Gedanke.

Übrigens muss an dieser Stelle auch eine enorme La-Ola-Welle an unsere Leser aus dem Bike- und Fahrrad-Lager rausgehen. Dass CURVES hauptsächlich aus der motorisierten, vierrädrigen Perspektive entsteht, ist kein Geheimnis. Mallorca hat für Fahrradfahrer den Status als Geheimtipp längst überschritten. Rennräder gehören hier vor allem in den milden Jahreszeiten zum ganz normalen Straßenbild. Wir haben verstanden, dass da zweierlei Dinge auf ein und derselben Straße passieren, die einen ähnlichen Genusskern haben: Autos und Fahrräder leben in unterschiedlich schnellen Paralleluniversen, der Rhythmus ist anders, das Timing und das Erleben. Eigentlich gehört gegenseitige Achtsamkeit ja ohnehin in das Repertoire eines jeden Verkehrsteilnehmers. Wer Geduld hat, mitdenkt und intelligent kommuniziert, erhöht für alle „soulful driver" nicht nur die Sicherheit, sondern vor allem den Spaß.

Und jetzt: Danke an die Mallorquiner. Wir Mallorca-Fans muten Ihrer Insel manchmal einiges zu. Dass wir immer noch das Gefühl haben, von Herzen willkommen zu sein, das ist eine ganz spezielle Eigenschaft der Mallorquiner und vielleicht einer der größten Momente der Beliebtheit Ihrer Insel.

Und Danke an Mallorca. Es macht Freude hier zu sein. Wir haben jede einzelne Kurve genossen, uns bemüht, all die Geschichten der Täler und Berge kennenzulernen, sind im Lauf von vielen Tagen unterwegs wirklich angekommen. Vielleicht ist diese Insel ja wirklich einfach nur ein toter Fels im Mittelmeer und unsere aufprojizierte Sehnsucht nach Zeitlosigkeit und Wärme macht sie zum Sehnsuchtsort. Es gibt aber Momente in den Bergen, in den Hügeln und der Ebene, in denen dieser Ort zu sprechen beginnt. Der Wind in den Klippen der Tramuntana hoch über dem Meer. Der Duft von Nadelbäumen in warmen Tälern. Das Klatschen von azurblauen Wellen in den kleinen „Coves" an der Felsküste. Die schweißüberströmte Hitze im Landesinneren am Mittag, wenn die Erde plötzlich mürben und wilden Geruch verströmt. Der Zeitlupen-Herzschlag der Klöster, Kirchen und heiligen Orte.

Und eines unserer Lieblings-Themen: das Essen auf Mallorca. Die Insel hat keinen kulinarischen Ruf. Und dabei haben wir hier so gut gegessen wie schon lange nicht mehr. Es ist also auch in dieser Hinsicht typisch für Mallorca: Ein zweites Hinsehen lohnt sich.

we know that it hasn't (always) been so for a long time. We make CURVES for you as well, because we feel understood by you. And that's a pretty good thought.

At this point, we must also send a huge Mexican wave to our readers from the biking and cycling fraternity. It's no secret that CURVES is created mainly from the motorised, four-wheeled perspective. It's also pretty widely known that we also have an almighty weakness for two-wheelers, especially those propelled by muscle power. Majorca has long surpassed the status of insider tip for cyclists. Especially during the milder times of year, racing bikes are a standard feature of the roads here. While we were making this issue of CURVES, we were once again inspired by the dynamism and fighting spirit of cycling just by watching it. We understood that two different things with a similar core of enjoyment are happening on one and the same road: cars and bicycles live in parallel universes travelling at different speeds. The rhythm is different, the timing and the experience. Actually, mutual awareness should be part of every road user's repertoire. If you have patience, think things through and communicate intelligently, it's safer and, above all, more fun for all "soulful drivers".

And now – thank you to the Mallorquins. Us fans of Majorca sometimes expect a lot from your island. That we still have the feeling of being warmly welcomed is a very special characteristic of the Mallorquins and perhaps one of the greatest moments of your island's popularity.

And thank you to Majorca. It is a pleasure to be here. We enjoyed every single curve, made the effort to get to know all the stories of the valleys and mountains and, during our many days on the road, we truly arrived. Perhaps this island really is just a dead rock in the Mediterranean and it is the yearning for timelessness and warmth we project onto it that makes it such a desirable place to be. But there are moments in the mountains, in the hills and on the plain when this place starts to speak. The wind in the cliffs of the Tramuntana high above the sea. The fragrance of pine trees in warm valleys. The splashing of azurblue waves in the small "coves" along the rocky coast. The searing midday heat inland when the earth's wild, mellow scent suddenly burst forth. The slow-mo heartbeat of the monasteries, churches and holy places.

And one of our favourite things – the food on Majorca. The island doesn't have a culinary reputation. Yet, we ate better here than we have in a long time. This, too, is typical for Majorca – it's worth a second look.

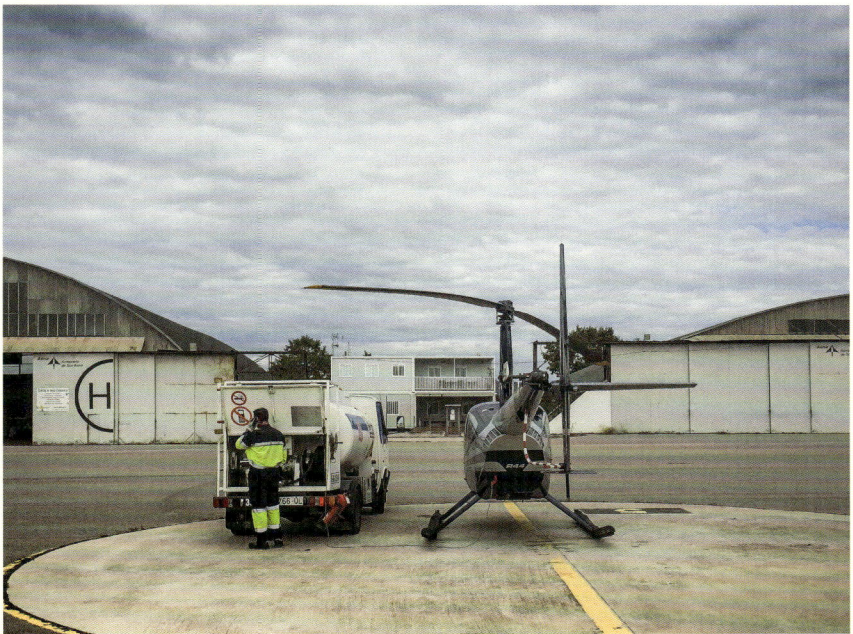

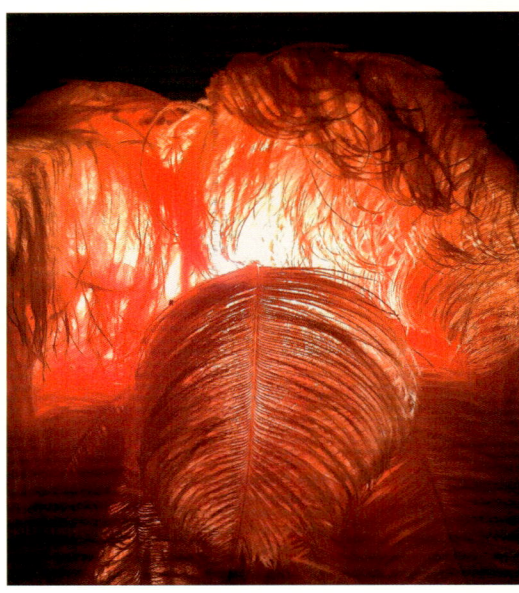

PUNKY

DANK AN / THANKS TO

MICHAEL DAIMINGER, BEN WINTER, NADJA KNEISSLER, JÖRN HEESE, HANNO VIENKEN, MICHAEL DORN, MICHAELA BOGNER, PHILLIP HOHENTHANNER, HEIKO WILD (BIKEDRESS), ALEX SPRINGER

SPECIAL FX / SPECIAL FX

BASTIAN SCHRAMM, LAURA KERN · ROTORFLUG - CEDRIC & PHILLIPE. CORNELIUS DORNIER UND MARTEN ROLFF FÜR DIE FOODTIPPS. DAVID & LOTTE!

Kraftstoffverbrauch/Emissionen* des Porsche Boxster GTS / Fuel consumption* Porsche Boxster GTS:

Kraftstoffverbrauch (in l/100 km)*: innerorts 11,5 · außerorts 6,8 · kombiniert 8,5; CO_2-Emissionen kombiniert 195 g/km
Fuel consumption (in l/100 km)*: urban 11.5 · extra urban 6.8 · combined 8.5; CO_2 emissions combined 195 g/km

Kraftstoffverbrauch/Emissionen* des Porsche Macan / Fuel consumption* Porsche Macan:

Kraftstoffverbrauch (in l/100 km)*: innerorts 9,5 · außerorts 7,3 · kombiniert 8,1; CO_2-Emissionen kombiniert 185 g/km
Fuel consumption (in l/100 km)*: urban 9.5 · extra urban 7.3 · combined 8.1; CO_2 emissions combined 185 g/km

* Die angegebenen Werte wurden nach dem vorgeschriebenen Messverfahren (§ 2 Nr. 5, 6, 6a Pkw-EnVKV in der jeweils geltenden Fassung) ermittelt.
* Data determined in accordance with the measurement method specified by Section 2 No. 5, 6, 6a of the German Ordinance on the Energy Consumption Labelling of Passenger Cars (PkW-EnVKV) in the version currently applicable.

IMPRESSUM / IMPRINT

HERAUSGEBER/
PUBLISHER: CURVES MAGAZIN
THIERSCHSTRASSE 25
D-80538 MÜNCHEN

VERANTWORTLICH FÜR
DEN HERAUSGEBER/
RESPONSIBLE FOR
PUBLICATION:
STEFAN BOGNER

KONZEPT/CONCEPT:
STEFAN BOGNER
THIERSCHSTRASSE 25
D-80538 MÜNCHEN
SB@CURVES-MAGAZIN.COM

DELIUS KLASING
CORPORATE PUBLISHING
SIEKERWALL 21
D-33602 BIELEFELD

REDAKTION/
EDITORIAL CONTENT
STEFAN BOGNER
BEN WINTER

DELIUS KLASING

ART DIRECTION, LAYOUT, FOTOS/
ART DIRECTION, LAYOUT, PHOTOS:
STEFAN BOGNER
FOTOS MAKING OF/
PHOTOS MAKING-OF:
MICHAEL DAIMINGER

TEXT/TEXT: BEN WINTER

TEXT INTRO/TEXT INTRO:
BASTIAN SCHRAMM

MOTIVAUSARBEITUNG
LITHOGRAPHIE/SATZ/
POST-PRODUCTION,
LITHOGRAPHY/SETTING:
MICHAEL DORN

KARTENMATERIAL/MAP MATERIAL:
MAIRDUMONT

ÜBERSETZUNG/TRANSLATION
ELAINE CATTON

PRODUKTIONSLEITUNG/
PRODUCTION MANAGEMENT:
JÖRN HEESE

DRUCK/PRINT:
KUNST- UND WERBEDRUCK
BAD OEYNHAUSEN

CURVES AUSGABEN / OTHER ISSUES OF CURVES

  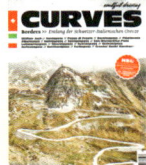     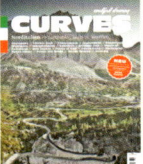 

PYRENÄEN
PYRENEES
Im Handel erhältlich/Available in stores

ÖSTERREICH
AUSTRIA
Im Handel erhältlich/Available in stores

SCHWEIZ
SWITZERLAND
Im Handel erhältlich/Available in stores

SCHOTTLAND
SCOTLAND
Im Handel erhältlich/Available in stores

FRANKREICH
FRANCE
Im Handel erhältlich/Available in stores

USA · KALIFORNIEN
USA · CALIFORNIA
Im Handel erhältlich/Available in stores

SIZILIEN
SICILY
Im Handel erhältlich/Available in stores

NORDITALIEN
NORTHERN ITALY
Im Handel erhältlich/Available in stores

DEUTSCHLAND/DÄNE.
GERMANY/DENMARK
Im Handel erhältlich/Available in stores